Celebrating Life as Grandparents

A Study Guide for Enriched Grandparenting

Roger Sonnenberg

CONCORDIA®

PUBLISHING HOUSE
3558 SOUTH JEFFERSON AVENUE
SAINT LOUIS, MISSOURI 63118-3968

Cover photos (left to right): Julie Marcotte/Tony Stone World Wide; Bob Taylor; Jim Whitmer; Skjold.

Edited by Thomas J. Doyle and Earl H. Gaulke
Pegi Minardi, Editorial Assistant

CONTENTS

So God created [grandparents] . . . [and] saw all
that He had made, and it was very good.

— *Genesis 1:27, 31*

Chapter 1

GRANDPARENTS?
WHO ARE THEY?

"ONE PICTURE IS WORTH A THOUSAND WORDS"

Children's children are a crown to the aged. (Proverbs 17:6)

AMA & PAPA IJAMES

About Ama and Papa Ijames

Jacob: This is my Papa, he makes toys for me, and he is nice to me. This is my Ama, Papa's friend and my "Ama" and friend.
Mommy: Why did you put yourself in the picture?
Jacob: Because I wanted to.

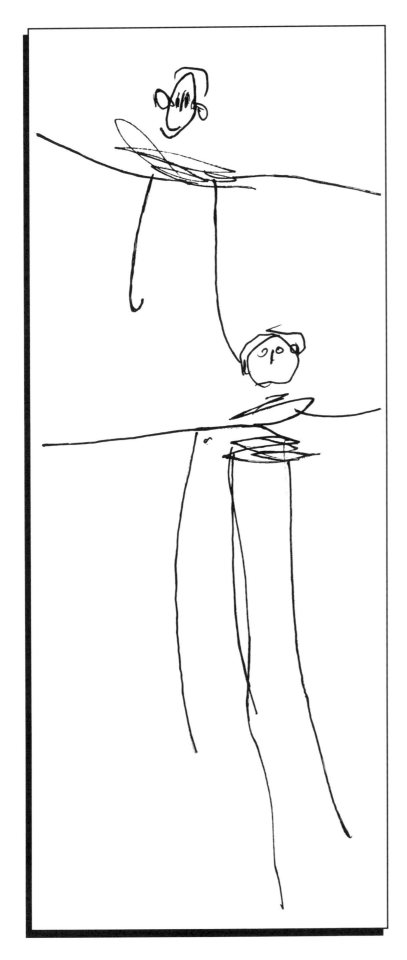

GRANDPA AND GRANDMA SONNENBERG

About Grandpa and Grandma Sonnenberg

Mommy: Why don't you draw a picture of Grandma and Grandpa Sonnenberg?

Jacob: I can't.

Mommy: Why not?

Jacob: Because I don't know what they look like!

Mommy: Here's a picture of them. Remember, last summer when we visited them on the farm?

Jacob: This is my Grandma with the short legs. She does all the work on the farm. This is Grandpa with the long legs. It is fun to feed the cows and pigs pickles with him.

GRANDMA EDNA

About Grandma Edna

Jacob: This is Grandma Edna. She is really nice to me and gives me lots of treats.

Jacob is four years old. Papa and Ama are his California grandparents. They live approximately three miles from him. Note the wide, happy, smiles on both Papa and Ama—and on Jacob!

1. How do you think Jacob feels about his California grandparents?

Both Papa and Ama are retired. Two days out of the week they baby-sit Jacob. This time is almost entirely devoted to Jacob. They do everything from baking cookies together to building model planes. Stories are read. They can be seen taking walks down Longden Avenue, hand-in-hand, with nature lessons being given by either Ama or Papa. Together they plant and harvest their garden.

2. Do you remember such times with your own grandparents? As time permits, briefly share remembrances with your group.

Grandpa and Grandma Sonnenberg are Jacob's long-distance grandparents. They live several thousand miles away in Minnesota. Jacob sees them once a year, in the summer. Thus, Jacob remembers Grandma as busy harvesting the garden produce. This explains why he sees Grandma as someone who does "all the work on the farm." Grandpa is also busy, but Jacob does not see his busyness since Grandpa is out on some distant field, mowing, raking, or baling hay.

3. What one "fun" thing does he remember doing with Grandpa?

4. Though he talks with Grandpa and Grandma Sonnenberg on the telephone, what significance is there in that he did not draw mouths on them?

5. Why do you think he did not include himself in the picture?

6. Do you think the size of Grandma Edna reflects Edna's importance in Jacob's life? Or does it reflect the "lots of treats" she gives him? Or both?

Grandma Edna is Jacob's surrogate grandmother. The large-sized picture represents the mental image Jacob has of her and how vital she is in his life. She lived with Jacob and his parents for two years while her condominium was being completed. This made Edna and Jacob very close.

7. Draw the picture you think your grandchildren might draw of you. (This might include several different pictures.) After drawing the picture(s), discuss in a small group the reasons for your drawing(s).

GRANDPARENTS AS "SILENT SAVIORS"

Defend the cause of the weak and fatherless; maintain the rights of the poor and oppressed. Rescue the weak and needy. (Psalm 82:3–4)

U.S. News & World Report's feature article for Dec. 16, 1991, was entitled: "Grandparents: The Silent Saviors." Statistics show that there are more than 3.2 million such "silent saviors" in the United States. They are "silent saviors" because they have had to assume the role of primary caregivers for their grandchildren, whose own parents have abdicated that responsibility for a whole host of reasons: separation or divorce, unemployment, alcohol or drug abuse, run-ins with the law, etc. The list is endless.

These "saviors" say:

"I knew I had to take the girls when my daughter looked at me and said, 'Just let me be a junkie.'"

"I believe the death of my daughter-in-law happened for a reason. I thank God for putting little Evetta into our lives. If she left us now, there would be a huge void."

"I try to explain about our finances, but it's hard for the girls [the grandchildren] to understand. At least when they go to bed at night, they know they're going to wake up in the same place."

(From *U.S. News & World Report*, 16 December 1991. Used by permission.)

Just as grandchildren need rescuing at times, so we need a rescue, a rescue from death and the power of the devil. We need a Savior who will rescue us from being a "junkie to sin." And thus, on Christmas Eve, God slipped down to earth to rescue the world. As Christians, we celebrate the fact that we have a "Savior."

1. Recall what the Savior's mission was according to Matthew 1:21.

2. Specifically, how did the rescue take place (Galatians 4:4–5)?

3. Celebrate together the accomplishment of the rescue mission in the words of the following litany:

> **Leader:** O God,
> **Participants:** our greatest lover,
> **Leader:** who so loved,
> **Participants:** to the greatest degree,
> **Leader:** who so loved the world,
> **Participants:** the greatest company,
> **Leader:** that He gave,
> **Participants:** truly, the greatest act,
> **Leader:** His one and only Son,

Participants: His greatest gift,
Leader: that whoever,
Participants: the greatest opportunity,
Leader: that whoever believes,
Participants: the greatest invitation,
Leader: that whoever believes in Him,
Participants: the greatest attraction,
Leader: shall not perish,
Participants: the greatest promise,
Leader: shall not perish but,
Participants: the greatest difference,
Leader: shall not perish but have
Participants: the greatest certainty,
Leader: eternal life,
Participants: the greatest possession.
Leader: Amen.
Participants: It shall be so.

THE CHANGING ROLES OF GRANDPARENTS

Israel said to Joseph, "I never expected to see your face again, and now God has allowed me to see your children too." (Genesis 48:11)

Some say grandparents aren't what they once were! With increased mobility many grandparents are simply not close at hand to do much grandparenting. With more and more divorces, many grandparents are separated from their grandchildren. And let's face it, grandparents of today do different things than grandparents of yesteryear. Some still choose to spin yarn or make apple pies. Others play golf at their Florida home-away-from-home! They're up early jogging or teaching aerobics to other grandparents. They don't have time to show off pictures of their grandchildren, because they're too busy dancing or taking classes at the local college.

In the dim and distant past
When life's tempo wasn't fast
Grandma used to rock and knit,
Crochet, tat, and baby-sit.

When the kids were in a jam,
They could always count on Gram.
In an age of gracious living,
Grandma was the gal for living.

Grandma now is at the gym
Exercising to keep slim.
She's off touring with a bunch,
Taking clients out to lunch.

Driving north to ski or curl,
All her days are in a whirl.
Nothing seems to stop or block her,
Now that Grandma's off her rocker.
—author unknown

10

And *yes*, surveys show that many grandparents simply choose to ignore their grandchildren!

According to an extensive survey by Arthur Kornhaber, M.D., a medical director of a pediatric neuropsychiatric group that treats children and their families in New York, only 5 percent of American children have close and regular contact with their grandparents. Another 5 percent never see grand-parents. But what disturbed Kornhaber most was the 70–80 percent of the grandparents who said that, while they dearly love the youngsters, they are seldom able or can bother to see the grandchildren more than once or twice a year.
("Where Have All the Grandparents Gone?" by Jay Stuller. Reprinted by permission, *The American Legion Magazine* [June 1984]. Copyright 1984.)

Considering some of the things you've just studied, describe your grandparenting to your group. (Your grandparenting style may even vary, depending on which grandchild you're talking about): Are you a long-distant grandparent? Are you a "silent savior" to one or more of your grandchildren? Do you live in close proximity to your grandchildren but far apart in a meaningful relationship? Are you close in proximity and in relationship?

THE IMPORTANCE OF GRANDPARENTING HASN'T CHANGED!

A good man leaves an inheritance for his children's children.
(Proverbs 13:22)

Though some grandparents may not want to be "bothered" by their grand-children, many others desire more than anything to be good grandparents—grandparents who positively influence their grandchildren. However, just as happy marriages and good parenting don't happen automatically, so good grandparenting doesn't just happen the day you receive the word you're a grandparent! Good grandparenting takes work. It takes planning. It means making a conscious decision to be involved in the life of the grandchildren (even if you're a long-distance grandparent). It means asking what kind of grandparents you'd like to be—or not be. In a small group, consider the following questions:

1. What kind of grandparent does God want me to be to my grandchildren (Deuteronomy 4:9; Titus 2:2–4)?

2. What kind of things about my belief and faith do I want to share with my grandchildren before I die?

3. What do I want to transmit to my grandchildren about our family culture and history?

4. What timeless truths would I like to share with my grandchildren before I die?

5. What kind of things would I like them to remember about me?

6. What kind of things would I like to do with them before I am unable to—or they don't want to?

7. In what ways should I support the grandchildren's parents? Verbally? Financially? Emotionally?

Excerpts from Letters of Grandparents

I'd like my grandchildren to know, more than anything, that I loved the Lord and that the Lord loved me . . . I'd like them to know Jesus so that we'll be a family in heaven just like we are here on earth.

I'd like my grandson to know the happiness of marriage as his grandmother and I knew. I'd like him to marry someone like his grandmother . . . someone who had her priorities in the correct order . . . someone who loved the Lord . . . someone who loved life . . . someone who knew how to laugh.

When so many people are so confused about so many things, we want you to know that there is really right and wrong. So many people may want us to believe that it's all a matter of situation or personal opinion, but that's just not so. There really are some basic moral laws in the world, laws given by God Himself. You've learned them as the Ten Commandments.

Look what comes with age!

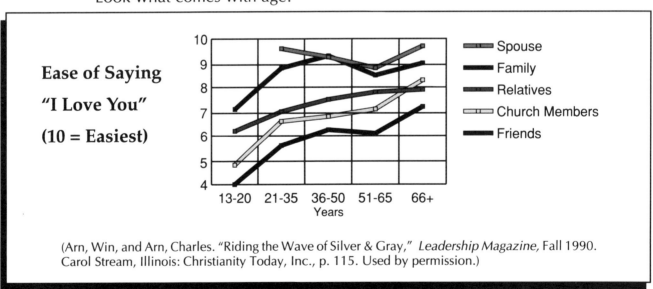

(Arn, Win, and Arn, Charles. "Riding the Wave of Silver & Gray," *Leadership Magazine,* Fall 1990. Carol Stream, Illinois: Christianity Today, Inc., p. 115. Used by permission.)

8. Which of these suggestions would you be willing to follow to help you be a better grandparent for your grandchildren?

a. Write each grandchild a special note this week, and in each note say, "I love you."

b. Talk to your children and ask them how you might be a better grandparent.

c. Record some of your family history on audio- or videotape this week for your grandchildren.

d. Write a special letter to your grandchild(ren). Tell your grandchild what you'd like him or her to remember about God.

e. Create a family tree. (See sample at the end of this chapter).

f. Plan a special occasion with your grandchildren. (See a movie together; go to a favorite pizza restaurant).

I believe that it is not dying that people are afraid of. Something else, something more unsettling and more tragic than dying frightens us. We are afraid of never having lived, of coming to the end of our days with the sense that we were never really alive, that we never figured out what life was for . . . Of all the fears that haunt us, from fear of the dark when we are young to fear of snakes and high places, there is nothing to compare to the fear that we may have wasted our lives with nothing to show for it.

(From *When All You've Ever Wanted Isn't Enough* by Harold S. Kushner. Copyright © 1986 by Kushner Enterprises, Inc. Reprinted by permission of Summit Books, a division of Simon & Schuster, Inc.)

CLOSING LITANY

Leader: Lord God, Your Word reminds us: "Children's children are a crown to the aged."

Participants: We thank You for the blessings of our children and our "children's children."

Leader: As they are "a crown," a gift, for us,

Participants: make us a gift to them.

Leader: For whatever type of grandparents we might be, grandparents close by, grandparents who are far away, grandparents who are "silent saviors,"

Participants: we pray, bless us, Heavenly Father. Help us. Make us wise in all that we do,

Leader: That we might "leave an inheritance" for them.

Participants: An inheritance which might bless each one of them,

Leader: but most especially, "an inheritance" which might further Your kingdom and bring You glory.

Participants: In the name of Jesus, who lives and reigns forever.

All: Amen. It shall be so.

Photos by Cleo Freelance

Grandparents are for telling you what it used to be like, but not too much.

— *Charlie Shedd*

Chapter 2

COMMUNICATING GRANDPARENTISH WISDOM

WISDOM? WHAT IS IT?

Be as wise as serpents. (Matthew 10:16 RSV)

There has been a tremendous explosion of knowledge over the last 50 years, and yet, with all the new knowledge, people seem to have more questions than ever. They know lots of things about things, but not much about life! They know about existentialism, but nothing about theism. They know about sex and birth control, but little about love and abstinence. The truth of the matter is though our children and children's children are bombarded with lots of knowledge, they have little wisdom!

There's a difference between knowledge and wisdom. Knowledge is being well-informed about factual matters, but knowledge is short-term. Wisdom is eternal.

According to The American Heritage Dictionary, wisdom is defined as "understanding of what is true, right, or lasting." Larry Lea in his book *Wisdom* defines that quality as "the God-given ability to perceive the true nature of a matter and to implement the will of God in that matter."

The Christian recognizes that what is "true, right, and lasting" can only be learned from God. Discuss with the person sitting next to you some of God's wisdom on the subject of wisdom:

1. Who is the source of wisdom according to Romans 16:27?

2. According to 1 Corinthians 1:30, who was the manifestation of God's wisdom?

3. After a lengthy discussion about wisdom in the book of Job, what conclusion is reached (Job 28:14–28)?

The best parent or grandparent is, therefore, the one who gets his or her wisdom from God.

This is what the Lord says: "Let not the wise man boast of his wisdom or the strong man boast of his strength or the rich man boast of his riches, but let him who boasts boast about this: that he understands and knows Me, that I am the Lord, who exercises kindness, justice and righteousness on earth, for in these I delight," declares the Lord. (Jeremiah 9:23–24)

4. Can your grandchildren see in you the type of wisdom described in James 3:17?

THE UNIQUENESS
OF GRANDPARENTISH WISDOM

The tongue of the wise brings healing. (Proverbs 12:18)

When we know about the past, we know more of how to live in the present and what we can anticipate about the future. Who can better witness about God's past blessings and love than grandparents? Who can better talk about enrichment gained through years of living than wise grandparents? Who can give life-messages better than wise grandparents?

Lewis B. Smedes writes in his book, *Caring and Commitment:*

A family is really a story, and a child's memory is a limited edition of his family's story. Every new generation writes a new chapter. But to write their own chapter, children have to know the chapters that went before theirs. This is why we need to hear about the olden days. We need a beginning for our own stories.

EARTHLY TRUTHS VERSUS HEAVENLY TRUTHS

But everyone who hears these words of mine and does not put them into practice is like a foolish man who built his house on the sand.
The rain came down, the streams rose, and the winds blew and beat against that house, and it fell with a great crash. (Matthew 7:26–27)

We gain knowledge in many ways—television, school, newspapers. However, what is sometimes given as knowledge is actually foolish and detrimental—emotionally, physically and spiritually. Some of the so-called truths are nothing more than lies. God prophesied of such times:

For the time will come when men will not put up with sound doctrine. Instead, to suit their own desires, they will gather around them a great number of teachers to say what their itching ears want to hear. They will turn their ears away from the truth and turn aside to myths. But you, keep your head in all situations . (2 Timothy 4:3–5)

These truths, concocted for our "itching ears," are packaged with some interesting slogans. Review the following slogans and discuss in small groups how you might share some grandparentish wisdom with your grandchildren regarding the truthfulness or deceptiveness of the slogan.

SLOGAN	QUESTIONS	TIMELESS TRUTHS I'D LIKE TO SHARE WITH MY GRANDCHILDREN
1. Everyone's doing it, so it's okay!	**a.** Have you heard your own children make this statement? or your grandchildren? What sins are sometimes excused with the argument, "Everyone's doing it, so it's okay"? **b.** What is God's reply to such an excuse in Romans 12:2?	
2. You only go around once, so live it up now!	**a.** Do you ever remember thinking this way during your lifetime? When? Who or what made you think differently? **b.** How does God describe the citizens of the world in Philippians 3:19?	
3. I love you, so let's have sex!	**a.** What was the prevailing philosophy about love and sex when you were younger? Were there any slogans floating around which described the prevailing sexual philosophy (e.g., "You made your bed, you'll have to sleep in it!"). **b.** Brainstorm some ways in which you might talk to your grandchildren about love and sex. **c.** What kind of things does God say in 1 Corinthians 6:18–20 and 1 Corinthians 13?	

4. Money talks, so earn as much as you can as fast as you can.

a. J. D. Rockefeller was once asked the question, "Just how much money is enough?" Rockefeller answered, "Just a little bit more." Agree or disagree?

b. After Rockefeller died, his accountant was asked, "Just how much did John D. Rockefeller leave?" He answered, "Everything!" Do you think this is one of those timeless truths you should share with your grandchildren? Is your own personal life reflecting such a belief?

c. Discuss the question asked in Luke 9:25.

d. Next time you read a story to your grandchild, read Luke 12:16–21.

5. All religions are essentially the same. We all worship the same God and are after the same thing.

a. Do you agree with any part of this present-day saying? Why?

b. Does God agree or disagree with the statement according to John 14:6 and Acts 4:12?

c. Discuss ways in which you might safely communicate, without alienating your grandchildren, God's truths to grandchildren who are being raised in the Mormon religion, or some other non-Christian religion.

6. Whoever heard of buying an automobile without trying it out first. So you don't get married without trying it out first to see if it works.

a. An increasing number of older adults live together without the benefit of marriage, sometimes for economic reasons. Is that a more justifiable reason for living together than the reasons many young people give for co-habitating.

b. Statistics show that the rate of divorce is actually higher for those who first live together, those who "try it out" first and then get married, as opposed to those who don't live together. Why might this be the case?

c. Do you think it is too old-fashioned, too grandparently, to teach abstinence before marriage or to advocate what God says in 1 Corinthians 6:18 and 1 Corinthians 6:9–10?

7. It can't be wrong 'cause it feels so good.

a. Study 1 Corinthians 6:12. What kind of feelings sometimes master people?

b. What kind of experiences might you share with your grandchildren about a time when your feelings led you astray? Why might it be helpful to share some of these mistakes with your grandchildren?

WHEN GRANDPARENTS AND PARENTS DISAGREE

I plead with Euodia and I plead with Syntyche to agree with each other in the Lord. (Philippians 4:2)

Every grandparent needs to be sensitive to different opinions which the grandchild's parent might have regarding child rearing. What may seem like grandparentish wisdom to you, might be unwise advice to the parents. In a small group discuss whether or not you agree or disagree with the following statements regarding grandparent-parent relationships:

1. Discuss with the parents what you're going to do for or with the grandchild before you actually do it (e.g., when you buy a special gift or the television programs the child's allowed to watch.)

2. When invited to a special event at the grandchild's house (e.g., a birthday party), make sure you let the parent be in charge, asking the parents, of course, if there's anything you can do to assist them.

3. Don't disagree over insignificant matters (e.g., whether or not the grandchild should have her ears pierced or whether or not she is allowed to sleep in on Saturday morning).

4. Never, never bad-mouth the parents in front of the grandchildren.

5. Support the parents, unless they advise their children in ways that are clearly contrary to Scripture, in which case, talk first to the parents about how their action violates Scripture and God's Law (e.g., the 15-year-old daughter is allowed to stay overnight at her boyfriend's house, in the same bed).

6. Affirm the parenting of the parents in front of the grandchildren.

SECRETS TO COMMUNICATING TIMELESS TRUTHS

My dear brothers, take note of this: Everyone should be quick to listen, slow to speak and slow to become angry. (James 1:19)

God not only gives us timeless truths to communicate, He also gives us secrets on how to communicate these truths. Discover from Scripture some of God's wise advice on communication by looking up the verses that follow and filling in the blank spaces. Discuss the question(s) that follow.

1. "Instead, speaking the _____ , we will in all things grow up into Him who is the Head, that is, Christ" (Ephesians 4:15).

Discuss some times when you might not have spoken the "truth in love" with your grandchildren?

2. "He who answers before _____—that is his folly and his shame" (Proverbs 18:13).

Parents don't always take time to listen. Televisions and videos don't listen to your grandchildren. They only spew out information. So who's left to listen to them? Maybe only God and you!

3. "A fool finds no pleasure in _____ but delights in airing his own opinions" (Proverbs 18:2).

Understanding takes time. You'll never know your grandchild's deepest secrets, his likes and dislikes, what makes him laugh or cry, unless you take time. Share what some of the "busy signals" sounded like when you were raising your own children. When you repeatedly receive busy signals, after trying to reach someone by phone, what do you eventually do? How are you going to avoid giving some of these same busy signals to your grandchildren?

4. "But while he was still a long way off, his father saw him and was filled with compassion for him; he ran to his son, _____

_____

_____."** (Luke 15:20).

Someone once said, "The greatest sense in our body is our touch sense. It is probably the chief sense in the processes of sleeping and waking; it gives us our knowledge of depth or thickness and form; we feel, we love and hate, are touchy and are touched, through the touch corpuscles of our skin."

What ways might you affirm your grandchildren through touch (e.g., holding hands)?

5. "_____ words are a honeycomb, sweet to the soul and healing to the bones" (Proverbs 16:24).

Words have great power. Advertisers pay millions of dollars to pay for a few seconds of advertising, because the words, few as they may be, convince people to buy, buy, buy! One New York advertising agency claims the three most powerful and most effective words in any advertising copy are: *new, improved,* and *free.*

An English professor compiled this list of words, which he believed are the most persuasive words in the English language: *money, discover, easy, health, proven, you, save, safety, love, results,* and *guarantee.* Of the 11 words, which two do you most often use with your grandchildren?

When you use the words *never* and *always,* are they used positively or negatively? Since both words often are exaggerations, do you think it is wise to use these words?

Do you think it's rude to spell out words in front of your grandchildren? (E.g., "Do you think we should tell him that his auntie d-i-e-d?")

6. "Where you go _____ ,

and where you stay _____ .

Your people will be my people and your God my God" (Ruth 1:16).

Good communication requires a secure and safe environment, meaning that someone can say what he or she thinks without the fear of being abandoned.

Often children of divorced parents are also divorced from one set of their grandparents. Every grandparent needs to know that even though parents may divorce one another, grandparents are forever! Our communication should reflect such assurance.

Good communication connects you to your grandchildren; it makes you present in their hearts and minds.

Could it be that for our children and our children's children, what we have to say is not nearly as important and memorable as the fact that we were there to say it?

"YIPPEE! I GOT A LETTER FROM GRANDMA!"

Realize that what we are in our letters when we are absent, we will be in our actions when we are present. (2 Corinthians 10:11)

"Yippee! I got a letter from Grandma!" exclaimed Jacob, as he tore open the letter he had just received from his grandmother Ijames. The special lollipop stuffed in the card dropped to the floor, as he begged his mom to read what the card said. One would think he had won the Publishers Clearing House $10 million prize as he listened attentively to the sweet words of his grandmother, written just for him. Jacob is always excited when he receives a letter in the mail, especially from one of his grandmothers.

Even with all the newest forms of communication available, letter writing is still one of the most popular. An advantage of communicating by mail is that letters, cards, and postcards can be read over and over. Though grandparents want to avoid "preachy" letters, letters afford grandparents, nearby and far away, an opportunity to share grandparentish wisdom. These letters can take on many different faces. For example, grandparents, whose grandchildren are too young to read, might communicate via a picture-letter. (Note the sample of one parent's picture-letter on page 25.)

Dearest Coleman,

It's not very often that I think about writing a letter to you. Even though I see you often, words seem more important when they're written on paper and can be kept forever. There are a few things I'd like to tell you that I hope you can remember.

First, I want you to know how precious you are to me! Your mommy was my last baby. God sent her to me as a wonderful surprise. As a little girl she was always a delight, and now that she's all grown up and a mother herself she has become my closest friend as well as a treasured daughter. From the time she was born I have always been so thankful that God chose me to be her mother. I have been enriched by every moment of her life, as will you. God has blessed her with many gifts and talents. You are fortunate to be her son because she can share so much with you while she lovingly guides you to manhood.

I remember the cold Dec. 22, eight years ago, when she walked into our home and introduced me to you, Coleman Ryan, six days old! I fell in love! I took you in my arms, looked into your deep blue eyes and saw the greatest wonder of all, my grandson. You reached up and caught my finger. I could feel your softly beating heart. A bond of love was born at that moment, and time eternal will not break it.

You're eight years old now, a young man enjoying second grade. The chubby baby I played with is long gone, but I have so enjoyed watching you grow. I've enjoyed the lunches we've had at McDonald's, the quarters I've given you to plunk into the surprise machines at the market, and the hours we've spent crouched on our knees on the living room floor, driving our Hot Wheels cars around the streets of our wooden block city. I happily remember the week you and your mommy shared our trailer, high in the Sierras. I loved making hot cocoa for a sleepy you, and I enjoyed our card games even if I could never beat you at Fish or Memory. You knew I always had cookies hidden away for you, and I loved watching Grampa teach you the safe way to use an axe and how to start a campfire with one match.

Someday I will have to leave you here and go home to the Lord. I hope that day is still many years in the future, but dearest Cole, whenever that day comes I will be leaving you with something special . . . just for you . . . that unique, wonderful love that only a grandmother can give, as well as all the precious memories that are ours alone.

Dearest Cole, please put this letter away some place and read it again when you are older. Remember that you are my much-loved grandson, and are one of the greatest joys in my life. I will keep you in my prayers and deep in my heart forever.

With all my love,

Your Grammie

Dear Meredith and Trevor,

Surprise! Surprise! Grandpa is writing a letter to you. Grandma and I usually take the easy way out and just pick up the telephone and dial. Not this time though.

Although you are more than 1,000 miles away, we want you to know you and your parents are in our hearts and prayers. We praise God daily that we are so very blessed with such beautiful, loving, Christian children and grandchildren.

We were so very pleased your mother brought you for a visit to California during your February semester break. We thank you for the wonderful time we had at Disneyland. It was truly a special day amid all the squeals of delight, the joy, laughter, and, of course, the screams as we repeatedly rode the mining train on Big Thunder Mountain.

Trevor, your dad told me you made your first basket in a recent league game. Congratulations! It must have been a special thrill to you. We are proud of you and your accomplishments in the soccer, basketball, and baseball leagues. I know one thing for sure; I will never have the eye and hand coordination to ever win a Nintendo golf game from you.

Meredith, how is everything going at the hospital? Are you still in the mother and baby care unit? We are very proud of your volunteer job as a candy-striper. It takes special loving and caring people like yourself to devote so much of your precious time to the welfare of others.

Grandma and I love you and your parents very much. We pray daily to Jesus that He will always watch over you and guide you in everything you do.

With all our love,

Grandma and Grandpa Michel

Dear Jacob:

Have Mommy and Daddy help you find on the map where we did these things.

XXOOXX

Grandpa

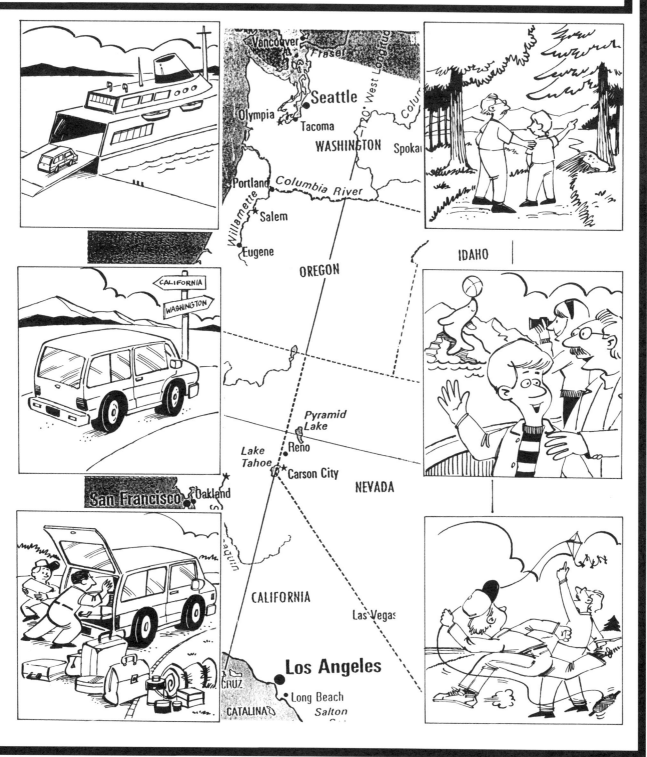

Turn to the person next to you and share how your grandparents most often communicated with you.

Part of a grandparent's privilege and responsibility is to pass on the wisdom, the eternal values, the things learned in the journey through life. Because we're all mortal, none of us will be around forever. Therefore, it is important we share important truths before it's too late. Letter writing is one such way to pass on these truths.

> # A challenge for the week:
> # Write each grandchild a special note, letter, or card!

There is good precedence for recording eternal truths in letters. God recorded many timeless truths in His epistles.

OTHER WAYS OF COMMUNICATING

They were talking with each other about everything that had happened. (Luke 24:14)

There are many ways to communicate grandparentish wisdom to your grandchildren. Here's one suggestion. In a smaller group, come up with at least two other ways you will communicate wisdom with your grandchild over the next few weeks.

1. Periodically send some special article you've clipped out of a newspaper or magazine or church newsletter. Grandchildren sometimes get the impression that grandparents do not know much about present-day problems. Show them otherwise. Ask the grandchild later what he thought of the article. Allow the article to serve as a springboard for communication. Be sure to listen to what he has to say about it before giving your opinion!

Two other ways in which I will communicate wisdom with my grandchildren:

2.

3.

"NOTHIN' SAYS LOVIN'
LIKE SOMETHING FROM THE OVEN"

Our forefathers ate the manna in the desert. (John 6:31)

In everyone's recipe box there are special handed-down recipes from a previous generation. Favorite family recipes tie families together from one generation to another. The Olson family gets together once a year, and family members bring favorite recipes along to the gathering. Someone collects the recipes, categorizes them, sends them away to a cookbook publisher, and upon getting the cookbooks back, makes sure that all who ordered a copy get one.

Here's a family heirloom recipe that's been passed on down to at least four generations. Grandma Esswein said this about the recipe: "This is 'the best' sugar cookie I have ever eaten—from the first four ingredients you can see why—they just melt in your mouth. My Mother, Edna (Wittland) Hempelman, who lived in Quincy, Illinois, gave this recipe to me when I was married over 43 years ago. Every time I make it, everyone wants the recipe. I don't know how old the recipe is, but since it makes eight dozen cookies, it was probably used for large families."

OLD-FASHIONED SUGAR COOKIES

1 cup butter	2 eggs
1 cup vegetable oil	1 teaspoon soda
1 cup granulated sugar	4 cups flour
1 cup powdered sugar	1 teaspoon cream of tartar
1 teaspoon vanilla	1 teaspoon salt

Preheat oven to 375 degrees. Thoroughly cream vegetable oil, butter, and both sugars. Add vanilla and eggs. Sift dry ingredients. Stir in and blend. Roll a teaspoon of soft dough into a ball. Roll ball in granulated sugar. Press down on lightly greased cookie sheet with a glass tumbler dipped in sugar. Press dough with fork to make design. Bake about 12 minutes. Makes eight dozen.

STOLLEN

3 1/2 cup milk
1/2 cup lukewarm water
2 envelopes yeast
10 cups flour
1 teaspoon salt
2 1/2 cup butter
1 1/2 cup sugar
2 teaspoons lemon rind

5 egg yolks
1 pound raisins (chopped)
1 pound nuts
1 pound citron
1/2 pound dates
1/2 pound cherries
1/2 cup confectioners sugar
1/2 ounce jigger of brandy

Scald the milk and cook to lukewarm. Dissolve the yeast in water for 10 minutes, add to milk. Add 6 cups flour and salt, mix to soft batter. Rise to double in bulk. Add 1 1/2 cup butter, sugar, lemon rind, and brandy. Mix thoroughly—add the remaining 4 cups flour, slowly working into mixture until it loosens from the sides. Now knead in the fruit and nuts, working in well. Divide into 5 or 6 parts, depending on size of loaf. Shape into long ovals and place in greased pan. Slash tops. Let rise until double in bulk. Bake at 350 degrees for one hour. After baked and partially cooled, use the rest of the butter in slashes on top. Then sprinkle with confectioners sugar. Store in a cool place.

Grandparents, why not make some sugar cookies or stollen for your grandchildren? If you don't have many grandchildren, invite your grandchildren's friends, because both recipes were for those days when they had much bigger families! Or why not make up a batch of sugar cookies and bring them to the next grandparenting class?

SHARING THE FAMILY HISTORY

Something grandparents can do better than anyone else is share family history. Unfortunately, grandparents don't always share what they know with their grandchildren, because the grandchildren don't seem very interested in it, until the grandparents have passed away. Wise grandparents should prepare for the day when grandchildren will want to know who their ancestors were and what they were like. Recording such information can be done in a variety of ways. With the advent of the video camera and the VCR, many grandparents are producing a video of the family history. Some grandparents prefer to share the family history through letters. Other families are much more precise and do it with meticulous charts. (Check your public library for a variety of books on researching and recording a family history.)

Draw as much of your family tree as you can remember.

SOME WISDOM AND WAYS TO TEACH IT

The weapons we fight with are not the weapons of the world.
On the contrary, they have divine power to demolish strongholds.
We demolish arguments and every pretension that sets itself up against
the knowledge of God, and we take captive every thought
to make it obedient to Christ. (2 Corinthians 10:4–5)

1. A failure in life is one who lives and fails to learn.
Model this truth to your grandchildren. Find out what hobby, club, or sport your grandchild is involved in. Go to the library and research the hobby, club, or sport. Share what you discovered with your grandchild.

2. More people would learn from their mistakes if they weren't so busy denying they made them.
Confide in your grandchildren that they're not the only ones who make mistakes. Share with them some of the mistakes you've made and what the consequences were. Be sure to tell them how God forgave you and how He kept you going despite your failures.

3. The man who says he's too old to learn new things probably always was.
We can learn much from our grandchildren about faith, about love, about giving and sharing, about life. However, in order to learn, we have to take time to listen. Begin by asking your grandchild what his or her favorite television program is. If you've never seen it, tune in when it's on, and make it a topic of your next conversation.

4. Adversity is never pleasant, but sometimes it's possible to learn lessons from it that can be learned in no other way.
Share with your grandchildren stories of things that happened in your lifetime that were not pleasant (catastrophes, tragedies, disappointments), but that taught you valuable lessons. "Now we see but a poor reflection as in a mirror; then we shall see face to face. Now I know in part; then I shall know fully, even as I am fully known" (1 Corinthians 13:12).

5. Learn from the mistakes made by others. You won't live long enough to make them all yourself.
Talk about some of the pain you experienced because of mistakes you've made. Assure your grandchildren that by sharing some of your painful experiences, you want to spare them of having to share the same.

6. You can buy education, but wisdom is a gift from God.
For many grandchildren, their grandparents are some of the wisest, smartest people around. Capitalize on this opportunity. Share your secret! "The fear of the Lord is the beginning of wisdom, and knowledge of the Holy One is understanding" (Proverbs 9:10).

7. True education enrolls men at the cradle and graduates them at the grave.

Therefore everyone who hears these words of mine and puts them into practice is like a wise man who built his house on the rock. The rain came down, the streams rose, and the winds blew and beat against that house; yet it did not fall, because it had its foundation on the rock (Matthew 7:24–25).

CLOSING LITANY

Leader: Lord God, thank You for this time together,

Participants: for making us wiser.

Leader: Forgive us, Lord God, for not always being wise in disseminating the wisdom You have given us in Your Holy Word.

Participants: Forgive us for not always communicating Your truth in love, for being too quick to speak, too slow in listening, too quick to get angry (James 1:19).

Leader: But thanks be to You, O Lord, for because of our faith in the life, death, and resurrection of Your Son Jesus, we know You assure us, "Though your sins are like scarlet, they [are] as white as snow; though they are red as crimson, they [are] like wool."

Participants: Thanks be to God.

Leader: Give us, Lord God, wisdom so that we might be wise communicatees to our children and children's children of Your wisdom, the wisdom of God;

Participants: so that our children and our children's children might be "like [the] wise man who built his house on the rock. The rain came down, the streams rose, and the winds blew and beat against that house; yet it did not fall, because it had its foundation on the rock."

All: Amen.

Grandpa Carl, Granmdma Linda and Cammi

Mark Munson and his niece, Cammi

Cammi and Marki

Mark Munson was 24 years old when he was murdered while walking his dog. Several months after his death, his sister named her newborn girl "Markie," after her brother Mark. At the hospital, after the doctors had come out of the emergency room to tell the family Mark had died, Mark's father told the family's pastor, "Pastor, I wouldn't be able to handle this if I didn't know Mark was with his Lord. Everything we've taught our children . . . everything we believe in, that Mark believed in, now has new meaning."

I will go to him,
but he will not return to me.

— *2 Samuel 12:23*

Chapter 3

LOVING AND SPOILING THEM — GOD'S WAY

"TO SPOIL?" WHAT DOES IT MEAN?

Like a city whose walls are broken down is a man who lacks self-control. (Proverbs 25:28)

Grandparents of yesterday as well as today are often accused of spoiling their grandchildren. When it is suggested to grandparents that they might possibly be spoiling their grandchildren, they respond in a variety of ways. Some just laugh about it. Others get defensive. Examine the responses of a few grandparents:

"I was too busy making a living to spoil my own children. Now that I'm retired, I've got the time, and I don't think I can spend it in any better way than with my grandchildren."

"We used to spend our money on essentials, like cars and making house payments. But now our priorities are different. We own our house! We have a nice bank account and the exact car we want! Our closets are filled. Our attic is filled with things we'll never use. We don't need anything for ourselves, so why not spend the money on our grandchildren?"

"Without even realizing it, my child grew up before I knew what happened. I'm not going to live what I've got left of my life and at the end discover it's gone without my knowing my grandchildren or them knowing me."

"Spoil? Why not? When we're through spoiling them, we can give them back to their parents and not have to deal with the consequences."

1. When you hear the word *spoil,* what comes to mind?

_____

_____

2. Write a definition of *spoil:*

_____

_____

Fred Gosman, in his best-selling book, *Spoiled Rotten*, gives the following satirical account of two parents arguing over who has the best equipped nursery:

> *"I just bought my child the best car seat," one parent brags. "It's anthropometrically designed" (whatever that means). "Terrific," her friend chimes in. "I just picked up a swing that doubles as a car seat and carrier, and a crib puff in tones of yellow and blue."*
>
> *"How nice," comes the icy reply. "By the way, did I tell you my baby's swing can run one hundred and fifty hours nonstop on two AA batteries? You still have to wind yours, don't you?"*
>
> *"Yes," says the embarrassed friend, "but Linda's swing is engineered to make a smooth, arc-like motion similar to my own, and her crib pillows play soothing lullabies."*
>
> *Bested at last, the irate mom loses all control. "Listen, you, your kid's musical mobile isn't voice activated, the receiving blanket has two torn appliques, and your high chair cover doesn't even match."*
>
> (From *Spoiled Rotten: Today's Children and How to Change Them.* © 1992 by Fred G. Gosman. Reprinted by Villard Books, a division of Random House, Inc.)

Though Gosman's conversation may be satirical, such conversations do take place. Too many parents and grandparents spoil their children and grandchildren. They stuff their nurseries full of every toy imaginable and pack closets with the latest in designer clothes. They plan elaborate birthday parties. And since no parent wants a child to suffer irreparable damage to his or her self-esteem because he or she does not have the right tennis shoes, the best are bought, despite the fact they cost three times more than the less popular, equally well-made brand.

3. One dictionary definition of *spoil* is "to overindulge." The opposite of overindulge is what we heard about in session 1. Do you think some grandparents, too busy with their own activities to see their grandchildren, try to compensate by overindulging their children with things?

4. God tells us that one of the fruits of the Holy Spirit is self-control. Self-control is like the brakes on a car. If the brakes on a car give out, what happens? In what ways might spoiling one's grandchildren with too many things be like losing the brakes on a car?

"BUT DOESN'T GOD SPOIL US?"

If you, then, though you are evil, know how to give good gifts to your children, how much more will your Father in heaven give good gifts to those who ask Him. (Matthew 7:11)

One grandfather, when he was accused of spoiling his grandchildren, snapped back, "Of course, I spoil my grandchildren! Every one of them! And

I have a good precedent for it. My heavenly Father spoils me all the time. Daily, He gives me more than I deserve! He plain, flat out, spoils me! If He can do it, certainly I can as well!"

1. Using the definition given by the man, is he correct in saying his "heavenly Father spoils" him? What if we use the definition given earlier—"to overindulge"; Doesn't God "overindulge" us, give us more than we deserve?

2. What do these verses say about our heavenly Father's behavior toward us?

a. Romans 5:6–8

b. Romans 6:23

3. Now consider the parable of the prodigal son in Luke 15:11–32:

a. Even though the prodigal son hadn't asked for forgiveness, what did the father do, according to verse 20?

b. What kind of things did the father "overindulge" the son with (vv. 22–23)?

A SCIENTIST AND HIS LITTLE PEOPLE

Once upon a time, there was a wonderful scientist who created little people, no more than just a few inches high. Some were fat. Some skinny. Some jolly. Some pretty with golden locks of hair. Some with great agility.

He placed them all into his laboratory sink, making what he thought was a perfect home for them. He provided everything they needed. He carefully controlled the sink's temperature. Recreation of all kinds was made available. "Rules for Happiness and Peaceful Living" were posted on the laboratory walls. No expense was spared in bringing in the very best food. For a while, everyone seemed to be happy.

But then the little people started to quarrel with each other. One liked the way the morning rays of the sun struck a part of the sink and wanted to move into that location, but the spot was occupied by someone else. He ordered him to move. They argued. Soon, another stole from his neighbor. Several started to gossip about how one woman snored so loudly that she woke up her neighbors. The little people started to take sides. They even started to fight with one another, until, one day, one killed another.

The scientist retired for the night, not knowing what to do. He had given his little people everything they needed. Frustrated and unable to sleep, he got up, went over to the laboratory sink and pulled the plug. He opened the faucet above and watched the water forcefully splash down into the sink. With tears in his eyes, he saw his little people wash down into the drain, saying, "I didn't want it this way. I didn't want it this way."

Why do you think our heavenly Father didn't do the same thing with the "little creatures" He created?

4. There's a wonderful story told by Jesus in Luke 11:7–11. The scene is late at night. The floor of a one-room house is covered with sleepers. Suddenly, loud knocking can be heard at the door. A weary traveler has come to a neighbor's house, hungry after a long journey. The neighbor has discovered he has no bread in the cupboard, and so he is knocking at his next-door neighbor's house. Bedlam begins to break loose. The once-asleep children begin to stir. The youngest begins to cry. Dogs start barking in the neighborhood as they too are awakened by the man's constant pounding. The half-asleep man of the house tries to quietly, but politely, shoo the man away. "Don't bother us. The doors are locked. The children are asleep. . . ." But the friend continues persistently. Begrudgingly, his friend gets up and gets him the food he asks for.

a. What heavenly truth is Jesus teaching in telling the earthly story in Luke 11:7–13 (also Matthew 7:11)?

b. Look carefully at Luke 11:9. Notice the word *it* in Christ's promise. What does "it" refer to? Could it be, He'll give us whatever is for our best? Review His promise of Romans 8:32.

c. What kind of spoiling might earthly fathers do which would not be for the child's well-being.

Earthly fathers sometimes spoil with things, failing to realize that material things do not by themselves create happiness.

SPOILING, GOD'S WAY

Love each other as I have loved you. (John 15:12)

"One of my favorite things to do with Grandpa is to go fishing."

"This was the day Grandpa and I dug up the olive tree. It was so big, but Grandpa and I did it. . . .
Were we tired when we got through!"

"We spent a whole week vacationing with Grandma and Grandpa!"

So how do we spoil God's way? Discuss the following suggestions with the person sitting next to you.

1. With One-on-One Contact

God spoiled us by loving us in person: "The Word became flesh and made His dwelling among us" (John 1:14). Jesus came to show us how much God loved His children and children's children.

We can also "spoil" our grandchildren—God's way—by loving them in person. Letters, telephone calls, gifts are wonderful, but they never replace a live body! Grandchildren need to see and touch their grandparents. Grandparents need to see and touch their grandchildren. Gary Smalley and John Trent, in *The Blessing* (Pocket Books,1986), discovered "that just to maintain emotional and physical health, men and women need 8–10 meaningful touches each day."

It is up to the grandparents to arrange for a time when such spoiling can take place. Why not arrange, a year in advance, a special vacation for just you and your grandchildren? (You may have to arrange several different times, depending on the number of the grandchildren you have.) After conferring with the grandchildren's parents and the grandchildren themselves, circle the date on your calendar. Make sure your grandchildren do the same. Whatever you decide to do on this special vacation, make sure it's something that will provide opportunity for individual time with your grandchildren.

A child loved to be read to every night. The father, being terribly busy, decided he would record many of the child's favorite stories, so that at night, the child could simply push the button on her tape recorder and hear her favorite story as many times as she wanted. It worked for a while, but late one night the little girl came to where her Daddy and Mommy sat watching television and said, "Daddy, I don't like these stories anymore. I want some with skin on them. Would you hold me, and read a real story to me tonight?"

2. With Letters and Notes

God wrote to His children. "All Scripture is God-breathed and is useful for teaching, rebuking, correcting and training in righteousness, so that the man of God may be thoroughly equipped for every good work" (2 Timothy 3:16–17).

We can let our grandchildren know how much we love them with our letters and notes. Staying in touch with letters, cards, and notes is especially useful if we're long-distance grandparents. If your grandchild is too young to read, send her a word-picture letter (by drawing pictures instead of using words). When you send your next letter to the family, why not write the letter to the grandchildren? Be assured, the parents will read it!

3. With Gifts

Jesus spoils His children with countless gifts: "Every good and perfect gift is from above, coming down from the Father of the heavenly lights, who does not change like shifting shadows." (James 1:17). Jesus doesn't always give His children what they want but always what they need, what is best for their well-being.

Many grandparents spoil their grandchildren with gifts. Gifts remind grandchildren they're special, that Grandpa and Grandma are thinking about them. Don't limit the gift giving to special holidays, and don't stop giving gifts just because they have reached a certain age. Most grandchildren in college welcome any kind of care package, especially if it contains goodies from Grandma.

You might ask the following questions whenever buying special gifts:

a. Will the gift meet with the parent's approval?

b. Is it age appropriate?

c. Can I afford the gift?

Recently a department store sponsored a promotion where young children could register to win a limousine ride to school on the first day. Do our first-graders really need limousine rides?

(From *Spoiled Rotten: Today's Children and How to Change Them.* © 1992 by Fred G. Gosman. Reprinted by Villard Books, a division of Random House, Inc.)

4. With Forgiveness

God spoils us with undeserved forgiveness: "God was reconciling the world to Himself in Christ, not counting men's sins against them" (2 Corinthians 5:19). It is forgiveness we don't deserve.

Grandparents need to forgive. Forgiveness, however, does not mean tolerance of wrongdoing. Despite the rose-colored glasses that grandparents sometimes wear when they look at their grandchildren, no grandchild is perfect. If the grandchild is visiting at your house and sets the dog on fire or sneaks out of bed to watch late-night cable TV after everyone's gone to bed, grandparents need to be honest enough to correct him or her. Grandchildren make mistakes. Good grandparents recognize it, administer the proper discipline, and offer forgiveness, just like God does with us.

"My grandma and grandpa live in Ohio so I never see them. They are still mad at my parents because we moved out to California. They thought we were abandoning them and the whole family. They still write to us, but they think that we are 'airhead Californians' with blond hair and no brains. They also think we are always on a diet." (Martin, age 10)

5. With Security

Jesus is always there for us: "Never will I leave you; never will I forsake you" (Hebrews 13:5).

Though distance or other commitments may not always allow us to be there in person, we can assure our grandchildren that we will be there when they need us, even if only via the phone. Grandchildren of divorced parents need to know that their grandparents haven't divorced them.

GRANDPARENTS

Grandparents are nice
as nice as they can be.

Grandparents are sweet,
as sweet as they can be.

Grandparents are smart,
as smart as they can be.

But the thing I really love
about grandparents is that they
are there for me.

David Granchukoff, grade 7

---

6. With Discipline

God loves us enough to say no: "Be careful to follow every command I am giving you today, so that you may live and increase and may enter and possess the land that the Lord promised on oath to your forefathers" (Deuteronomy 8:1).

Grandparents need to love enough to say no, no to things that are wrong, especially in God's eyes. Tolerance of evil is itself evil. Grandchildren will much more respect grandparents who have principles and values than those who are so wishy-washy that they don't believe in anything.

7. With a Hopeful Future

God showers His children with promises for tomorrow: " 'For I know the plans I have for you,' declares the Lord: 'plans to prosper you and not to harm you, plans to give you hope and a future.' " (Jeremiah 29:11–12).

No one can share firsthand experience of how God cares for His people better than grandparents, how He cared for them in the past, how He cares for their present needs, and how He will take care of their future needs.

CLOSING LITANY

Leader: Lord God, we acknowledge, if we who are evil, know how to give good gifts to our children, how much more will You give good gifts to those who ask! (Matthew 7:11)

Participants: Thank You, dear Father,

Leader: for spoiling us with the presence of Your Only-begotten Son, who came to earth to rescue faithless humanity through His life, death, and resurrection.

Participants: For more than we deserve, we thank You.

Leader: For loving us with Your Holy Word, which tells us of the way of salvation and how to have life more abundant,

Participants: for more than we deserve, we thank You.

Leader: For blessing us with countless gifts,

Participants: for more than we deserve, we thank You.

Leader: For loving us with forgiveness provided through Jesus,

Participants: for Your forgiveness for the times we have spoiled our children and our children's children in the wrong ways with the wrong intentions, we thank You.

Leader: For providing us with security, the security of knowing You will never leave us, never forsake us,

Participants: thank You, dear Father.

Leader: For loving us enough to discipline us,

Participants: thank You, dear Father.

Leader: For giving us the hope of a tomorrow, of a promised future;

Participants: thank You, dear Father.

Leader: Guided and empowered by You, Lord God, make us the type of parents and grandparents who give to our children and our children's children in a way that will reflect the way You give to us.

Participants: Make us generous in our giving,

Leader: but not foolish.

Participants: Make us loving but always wise,

Leader: like You, dear Father.

All: Amen. It shall be so.

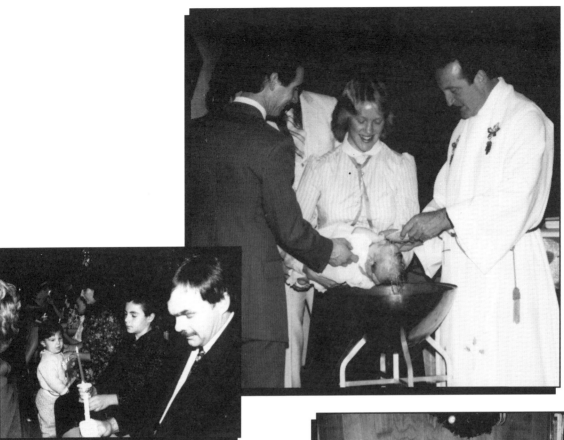

It is only when you teach your child how to die that you teach him how to live.

Chapter 4

GIVING THEM A TASTE OF GOD

WORDS THAT MADE A DIFFERENCE

The Sovereign Lord has given me an instructed tongue. (Isaiah 50:4)

Sarah Kathleen Blair

A moment shared by Sarah and her grandma

Michael and Eleda Blair, like many couples, could not have children, and so they sought to adopt. However, they soon realized what so many adoptive couples discover. Because of the many abortions, there are very few infant children available for adoption.

Through the help of their pastor they contacted a Christian lawyer who handled private adoptions. They submitted the necessary papers and a resume and waited.

43

Thousands of miles away in Texas, a life had begun in the womb of a teenage girl. The teenager, upon finding out she was pregnant, began inquiring how she might best take care of the unwanted pregnancy. Daily she struggled, and, after counseling with her peers and parents, made the decision to abort the baby. She made arrangements for the abortion at a nearby Planned Parenthood Clinic.

Back in San Diego, California, the teenager's aunt had tuned in to hear one of her favorite Christian broadcasts, "Focus on the Family," with Dr. James Dobson. The discussion was on the tragedy of the millions of abortions that take place each year. A Christian lawyer who specialized in arranging adoptions was also on the program. The fact that 1.5 million unborn children are aborted each year disturbed her greatly, so much so, she found it difficult to sleep that night. Even after she fell asleep, she had a strange dream. She dreamed her sister, living in Texas, was pregnant and planning to have an abortion.

The dream haunted her for several days, and, even though she knew her sister was unable to have any more children, she called her sister and told her about the strange dream. Her sister assured her that she was not pregnant but that her daughter was and that she was planning on having an abortion. The aunt shared what she had heard on the Christian program and asked that her sister talk to her daughter about the option of adoption.

The mother shared with her daughter what her aunt had told her, but, nevertheless, the teenager proceeded with plans for an abortion. However, as she and her sister were driving to the abortion clinic, the teenager began to cry and asked that her sister pull to the side of the road. She confessed to her sister that she couldn't go through with the abortion. They returned home.

After several days of wavering back and forth on what to do with her unborn baby, she called her aunt and asked if she could move to California to live with her during her pregnancy. The aunt agreed. She also asked if the aunt would make arrangements for an appointment with the Christian lawyer she had heard on the Dobson program.

Upon arriving in California, the unwed teenager met with the lawyer, and talked with him about the option of adoption. After discussion, the teenager decided to put her baby up for adoption. The lawyer presented her with resumes of people who sought to adopt. One of the resumes was that of Michael and Eleda Blair. After meeting with some of the potential adoptive couples, she selected the Blairs.

On July 9, 1989, the teenage mother handed the Blairs the gift of a child—Sarah Kathleen.

The miracle began because a Christian counselor was bold enough to talk about the tragedy of abortion and about an alternative—adoption. It took place because an aunt was bold enough to talk to her sister about what she had heard and what she thought God wanted her niece to do. Indiscriminate of borders, oblivious to all the other human impossibilities, God worked one of

His many miracles. It took place because God moved a frightened, unwed teenager to place her unborn child into the hands of a loving Christian family instead of an abortionist.

With a few words, boldly and faithfully spoken, a human life was spared!

BUT LIFE IS SHORT!

I wanted to see what was worthwhile for men to do under heaven during the few days of their lives. (Ecclesiastes 2:3)

A few words may have saved Sarah Kathleen, but for Sarah Kathleen, earthly life is still short.

1. What does James remind us of in James 4:14b?

	1950	1985	2020
POPULATION			
AGES 65—84 (in millions)	11.7	25.8	44.3
85 and over	0.6	2.7	7.1
65 and over as % of total population	7.7%	12%	17.3%
LIFE EXPECTANCY			
Total	68.2	74.7	78.1
Male	65.5	71.2	74.2
Female	71.0	78.2	82.0
Black	60.7	69.5	75.5
White	69.0	75.3	78.5
FEDERAL SPENDING			
Pension and helath-care payments as % of GNP	1.6%	9.3%	11.8%

(Copyright 1988 Time Inc. Reprinted by permission)

2. Even at best, what's the life expectancy for Sarah Kathleen according to the chart above?

A FEW WORDS CAN DO MORE THAN GIVE 78 YEARS OF LIFE

What good is it for a man to gain the whole world, yet forfeit his soul?
(Mark 8:36)

A few words can do more than give 78 years of life to someone. The right words spoken and believed can actually give someone an eternity!

1. What do the words of Scripture do according to St. Paul in his letter to Timothy (2 Timothy 3:15)?

2. Who shared these life-saving words with Timothy (2 Timothy 1:5)?

3. Describe the kind of parents (and grandparents) talked about in Deuteronomy 4:9 and 6:1–2.

Karen Carter is 106 years old. She lives alone. Though she needs a wheelchair and crutches to get around in her small trailer, she is "fiercely independent . . . 'There aren't too many things I can do these days,' Carter says, referring to the infirmities of aging—broken hips, failing eyesight, lapsing memory and a heart condition, the latter which she treats nightly with her own remedy: two teaspoons of Jim Beam in a half-glass of water. 'But as long as I can do this,' she says, wiggling her thumb, 'I can pray for people.' . . . The prayer warrior . . . prays for a Pasadena couple trying to have a baby; for an East Los Angeles woman whose son, a gang member, is doing time in prison; for a 40-year-old Burbank man dying of AIDS."
(Copyright 1992, *Los Angeles Times*. Reprinted by permission)

4. Every grandparent, long-distant or nearby, has the privilege and the responsibility to help their grandchildren taste God. No one can help children know more about the Lord than godly grandparents. Why? Because they have lived more of life than the grandchildren or their parents. They're closer to the finish line, and because of it, they have a clearer perspective of what the scenery is like along the way. They have much to share about the past, present, and the future.

Spend a few minutes, during class or some time this week, to reflect on your past, present, and future and the part God played, plays or will play in each.

a. When I think of my past, I think of how God . . .

b. When I think of the present, I think of how God . . .

c. When I think of the future, I think of how God . . .

List some of the important spiritual truths you hope each of your grandchildren will know about

- God;
- Jesus Christ;
- the Bible;
- sexuality;
- the church.

SPECIFIC WAYS TO HELP GRANDCHILDREN TASTE GOD

Impress them on your children. Talk about them when you sit at home and when you walk along the road, when you lie down and when you get up. (Deuteronomy 6:7)

A group of grandparents were asked, "In what ways do you convey spiritual truths to your grandchildren?" They suggested 10 different ways. Discuss the suggestions with the person sitting next to you.

1. THROUGH READING

"I have always loved reading books. I've passed on that love to my grandchildren by reading whenever I baby-sit them or whenever they come to visit at our house. Reading is my way of conveying wonderful religious truths to my grandchildren, because many of the books we read together are religious. One of my grandchildren, J. C., has heard the Mary Manz Simon's *Hear Me Read* Bible stories so often, he can now read them to me, and he's only in kindergarten."

Mary Manz Simon has written a series of books, published by Concordia Publishing House, that are a must in every grandparent's library. Each *Hear Me Read* book contains a well-known Bible story written in 25 words or less for a cost of approximately $2. They are books for children 2 years and up. They are beautifully illustrated.

2. THROUGH MODELING

"We have a very close relationship with our grandchildren. We see them often. Instead of lots of preaching, we try to behave a certain way, modeling a Christ-like life. We do lots of different things with them. Our daughter's children don't have their father living with them; in fact, they rarely see him, so they treasure spending time with us, especially Grandpa."

If a child lives with criticism,
    He learns to condemn.
If a child lives with hostility,
    He learns to fight.
If a child lives with ridicule,
    He learns to be shy.
If a child lives with shame,
    He learns to feel guilty.
If a child lives with tolerance,
    He learns to be patient.
If a child lives with encouragement,
    He learns confidence.
If a child lives with praise,
    He learns to appreciate.
If a child lives with fairness,
    He learns justice.
If a child lives with security,
    He learns to have faith.
If a child lives with approval,
    He learns to like himself.
If a child lives with acceptance
    and friendship,
    He learns to find love in the world.

(Nolte, Dorothy Law, "Children Learn What They Live," quoted by Jorie Kincaid in, *The Power of Modeling.* Colorado Springs, Colorado: Navpress, 1989.)

3. THROUGH SUNDAY SCHOOL AND CHURCH

"Our children don't seem to have time to take the children to Sunday school and church, but they don't object if we do. So we do!"

4. THROUGH CHRISTIAN DAY SCHOOL

"We help pay part of the parochial school tuition for our grandchildren. We not only help support them financially, but we also support them by being at many of the special functions they have at school, like at our grandson's basketball games or our granddaughter's plays."

Bernard and Renata Hartley travel more than 150 miles each Sunday to take their granddaughter Jessica to church and Sunday school.

5. THROUGH SPECIAL RELIGIOUS GIFTS

"Sometimes we buy our grandchild the toy everyone's getting their grandchild. However, along with the more popular gifts, we give religious gifts, such as when we gave him his first cassette player. It was one of those special children's recorders which you can't break. Along with the cassette player we gave him special Christian music cassettes! He loves both the cassette player and the cassettes. His mom tells us he plays the cassettes every night before going to bed."

6. THROUGH PRAYER

"Prayer has always been important to us. We have prayer lists which we post every week on the refrigerator door. Every week we place our grandchildren on the list. When our grandchildren visit, they always go to the refrigerator door to see if we're still praying for them."

7. THROUGH THE USE OF "TEACHABLE MOMENTS"

"We don't see our grandchildren but maybe twice a year. When we do see them, we try to take advantage of every opportunity to share our Christian beliefs. Quite often, our times together are around the holiday seasons. If it's Christmas time, we always try to make time when we talk about the real meaning of Christmas."

8. THROUGH SPECIAL NOTES/CARDS/LETTERS

"My grandchildren know that every time they receive a letter or note from me, it's going to have a few words about the importance of Jesus."

Dear Justin:

I enjoyed talking to you on the telephone yesterday and hearing about your wonderful day at the Indio Date Festival. What a great mom you have to take you and Katie on such a fun trip. You are having so many happy experiences that will be happy memories later. As you grow up, the experiences will be even more challenging to you, and your memory bank will grow!

Your mom told me how much you helped her with taking care of Katie, and in that way *you* are giving Katie happy memories of you. It reminds me of when your mom was little, and since she was the oldest of the children, she took good care of her little brother and sister, too. Did you know that she taught Uncle Jeff and Aunt Suzy to read? How wonderful I feel knowing that the good things continue in your generation. As a matter of fact, you are a perfect example of the wise words from the book of Proverbs in the Bible—"Train a child in the way he should go, and when he is old, he will not turn from it." Your mom was brought up to love and help her brother and sister, and now that she is grown, she is encouraging you to do the same thing. And you will remember when you are grown and have children of your own!

I am looking forward to visiting you in Palm Desert next week! I hope we will be able to go ice skating, and of course, we'll be able to swim in your pool and enjoy the warm sunshine! While your dad and Grandpa are fishing in Mexico, you will be the "man of the house."

Do you like getting letters? Now that you are learning to read and write, perhaps you can write me a letter. I would love to get a letter from you, or even just some of your pictures, because you draw very well. If possible, I'd like to get a picture from you of your idea of what Grandma and Grandpa look like—or showing some of your memories of times we have spent together. I will bring some cardboard to Palm Desert for you to draw on. Enclosed is some stationery for you to use for letters if you would like.

I like to write to you. It is a way of telling you how much I love you and how proud I am of you.

Love,

Grandma Ann

P.S. You know, I like to write stories, and I have enclosed some stories I wrote for Ryan and Glorianne, as well as another copy of the story I wrote for you.

9. THROUGH A GROWING FAITH

"We can't give to our grandchildren what we ourselves don't have. Therefore, we spend an hour each morning studying the Bible. Since we baby-sit our four-year-old grandson every day, we tell him it's time for Bible study for Grandma and Grandpa. He's gotten so that he now asks if he can join us. His mom packs his Bible every morning, so he feels like he's really a part of the study. Needless to say, his attention span is short, but we always enjoy having him, for however long."

Two outstanding orators entered a prestigious declamation contest. Both were asked to recite the Twenty-third Psalm. The first orator had a deep, resonant, baritone voice. He spoke the psalm, carefully enunciating each word and phrase with perfect timing. The second orator was more timid and less polished. Nevertheless, he won the contest. The judges declared him the winner, because they said, "He said the psalm as if he really believed the words!"

10. THROUGH LOVING THEM UNCONDITIONALLY

"Children today are being bombarded with all kinds of love, but it is love which is often conditional. We let our grandchildren know they're loved unconditionally, just like their heavenly Father loves them unconditionally."

"Dear friends, let us love one another, for love comes from God. Everyone who loves has been born of God and knows God" (1 John 4:7).

TAKING ADVANTAGE OF LIFE'S CHANGES TO TEACH VALUABLE SPIRITUAL LESSONS

Consider it pure joy, my brothers, whenever you face trials of many kinds. (James 1:2)

Often, there are noticeable physiological changes that accompany age, but instead of bemoaning these changes, turn them into something to help teach important spiritual truths.

True or False

1. Most older people need less sleep than younger people.

True. In sharp contrast to newborns, who need approximately 16–18 hours of sleep per day, most people by age 65 need less than 6 hours of sleep per day. As opposed to popping sleeping pills, why not spend the extra time writing notes of encouragement to your grandchildren? Or studying the Bible? Or praying for your grandchildren?

2. As one ages, the senses begin to deteriorate.

True. Hearing begins to fade. Around age 40, sight usually begins to deteriorate. Food doesn't taste like it used to. The sense of smell diminishes.

Why not tell your grandchildren you'd like to start a special college fund for them. The only condition is they have to earn it. Tell them you'd like to hire them for special tasks you can no longer do, such as read the Bible to you for 15 minutes each day.

3. Lungs lose breathing capacity.

True. Older people can lose up to 50 percent of their breathing capacity.

Exercise helps everyone maintain his or her health, including the health of older people. Why not join a health club? Instead of going to the club alone, why not get a family membership, and invite your grandchildren to join you? Studies show many of our nation's young people are out of shape and in need of exercise. Why not use the time to keep up your physical well-being—and your grandchild's, too. And as you exercise together, improve your spiritual well-being, too. Use the time together as an opportunity to talk about aging. Use it as an opportunity to talk about how God wants us to take care of our bodies. Take advantage of those "teachable moments" together to share God's wisdom.

WHAT ARE YOU TEACHING YOUR GRANDCHILDREN WHEN . . .

I thought, "Age should speak; advanced years should teach wisdom."
(Job 32:7)

Think about or discuss the following in your small group:

What are you teaching your grandchildren . . .

1. when you drop them off for Sunday school but don't go to Bible class yourself?

2. when you talk about your past but never about your present religious experiences?

3. when the only time you discuss God is when they've done something wrong, and you use God-language to try to get them to modify their behavior?

4. when you criticize the church you worship in or that your grandchildren worship in?

5. when you demand they say "I'm sorry" when they do something wrong, but don't demand the same of yourself when you do something wrong?

6. when every time they see you, you preach to them?

7. when you never talk about God except on your way to or from church?

8. when you preach one thing to the grandchildren but do something else?

9. when your Bible is filled with mementos of the past (e.g., old bulletins, clipping from magazines, dried flowers) but never opened for reading and study?

THE ULTIMATE QUESTION

But these are written that you may believe that Jesus is the Christ, the Son of God, and that by believing you may have life in His name.
(John 20:31)

Death is inevitable! Because it is, the question we must all answer is this, "What happens to me when I die?"

Max Lucado tells the touching story of being called to the bed of his dying father:

His head was all he could turn. Lou Gehrig's disease had leeched his movement, taking from him everything but his faith . . . and his eyes.

. . . Next to his bed was a respirator—a metronome of mortality that pushed air into his lungs through a hole in his throat. The bones in his hand protruded like spokes in an umbrella. His fingers, once firm and strong, were curled and lifeless . . . I stroked his hair.

"What is it, Dad?"

He wanted to say something. His eyes yearned. His eyes refused to release me. If I looked away for a moment, they followed me, and were still looking when I looked back.

"What is it?"

I'd seen that expression before. I was seven years old, eight at the most. Standing on the edge of a diving board for the first time, wondering if I would survive the plunge. The board dipped under my 70 pounds. I looked behind me at the kids who were pestering me to hurry up and jump. I wondered what they could do if I asked them to move over so I could get down. Tar and feather me, I supposed.

So caught between ridicule and a jump into certain death, I did the only thing I knew to do—I shivered.

Then I heard him say, "It's all right, son, come on in." I looked down. My father had dived in. He was treading water awaiting my jump. . . .

So I jumped.

Twenty-three years later the tan was gone, the hair thin and the face drawn. But eyes hadn't changed. They were bold. And their message hadn't changed. I knew what he was saying. Somehow he knew I was afraid. Somehow he perceived that I was shivering as I looked into the deep. And somehow, he, the dying, had the strength to comfort me, the living.

I placed my cheek in the hollow of his. My tears dripped in his hot face. I said softly what his throat wanted to, but couldn't. "It's all right," I whispered. "It's going to be all right."

(Excerpted from the book, *Six Hours One Friday* by Max Lucado [Sisters, Oregon: Questar Publishers, Inc.], 1989. Copyright 1989 by Max Lucado.)

Jesus says, "It's all right! Don't be afraid of death."

"I am the resurrection and the life. He who believes in Me will live, even though he dies; and whoever lives and believes in Me will never die" (John 11:25).

Copy Romans 6:23, and the next time you're with your grandchildren, memorize it together.

_____

_____

_____

_____

_____

_____

The greatest thing you can teach your grandchildren is the answer to life's ultimate question.

CLOSING LITANY

Leader: Lord God, You have given the promise,

Participants: "For God so loved the world that He gave His one and only Son, that whoever believes in Him shall not perish but have eternal life."

Leader: Though we confess the promise to be true, we also confess we're not always bold to proclaim this truth to our children and children's children as You tell us:

Participants: "These commandments that I give you today are to be upon your hearts. Impress them on your children. Talk about them when you sit at home and when you walk along the road, when you lie down and when you get up. Tie them as symbols on your hands and bind them on your foreheads. Write them on the doorframes of your houses and on your gates."

Leader: Forgive us Lord,

Participants: "For the wages of sin is death, but the gift of God is eternal life in Christ Jesus our Lord."

Leader: In the days and weeks and months ahead, give us the opportunities and the boldness to help our children and children's children taste God's love.

Participants: For "What good is it for a man to gain the whole world, yet forfeit his soul?"

All: Amen. It shall be so.

Grandpa's Charm

Wherever he goes,
Wherever he's at,
The thing I love most is to sit on his lap.
For he picks me up into his arms.
Mom calls it "grandpa's charm!"
But all I know is he's got loving arms.
I think it's okay to be old and grey,
'Cause he stops with me and he plays.
When I look for him I find him there.
I just look for grandpa's chair.
I'm so glad that he cares.
There's other grandmas and grandpas,
If you don't have one of your own.
They want to reach out their loving arms.
They'll make you feel right at home,
'Cause at times we all feel alone.
I'm going to see grandpa in heaven someday.
I can just see him waiting there.
He'll run and pick me up again.
Mom calls it "grandpa's charm."
But all I know is he's got loving arms.

Mary Rice Hopkins

Chapter 5

CREATING A HEALTHY CONGREGATIONAL CLIMATE

A CELEBRATION OF YOUTH

Don't let anyone look down on you because you are young.
(1 Timothy 4:12)

We live in a country that celebrates youthfulness; thus, we will do whatever it takes to fool ourselves and others into believing that we are still young. We change wives and husbands, clothes and faces in order to convince ourselves age hasn't caught up with us. We undergo painful surgery to get rid of the bags under our eyes, our faces lifted, and hair transplanted onto our heads. The drugstore shelves are lined with hair-coloring products for men and women. We do it because we want to be a part of the adored, the admired, the ones getting the most out of life.

Ageism can be seen as a process of systematic stereotyping of and discrimination against people because they are old, just as racism and sexism accomplish this with skin color and gender. Old people are categorized as senile, rigid in thought and manner, old-fashioned in morality and skills. . . Ageism allows the younger generations to see older people as different from themselves; thus they subtly cease to identify with their elders as human beings.

(Reprinted with permission of Macmillan Publishing Company from _Aging and Mental Health_: Positive Psychosocial and Biomedical Approaches, Fourth Edition by Robert N. Butler and Myrna I. Lewis. Copyright © 1991 by Macmillan Publishing Company.)

There used to be a time when the elderly were treated with respect and reverence. But times have changed. Now the elderly are pictured as liabilities. They are, too often, accorded second-class citizenship.

If society's negative attitudes toward the elderly are deplorable, unfortunately there is proof that professional attitudes of physicians, nurses, social workers, lawyers, and therapists, among others, are often negative, resulting in differential care. For example, it has been found that elderly clients, patients, or residents (within institutional settings) are often provided with inferior care and treatment by professionals. This is true for nonprofessionals as well. . . . Negative attitudes toward the elderly can be seen in the extent to which they are victims of crime. Butler indicates that old people, more so than any other age group, are victims of violent crimes such as vandalism, physical attacks, *theft, and robbery. In addition, the elderly are preyed upon by those engaged in fraud and confidence schemes which promise quick cures or easy profits . . . Loneliness makes them attractive and gullible victims for "sympathetic" and "friendly" conartists and deceptive salespersons.*

(Reprinted with permission of Macmillan Publishing Company from *Aging and Mental Health*: Positive Psychosocial and Biomedical Approaches, Fourth Edition by Robert N. Butler and Myrna I. Lewis. Copyright © 1991 by Macmillan Publishing Company.)

The lack of respect and reverence for life, especially any life which may prove to be a liability, has taken place gradually over the last 50 years. This lack of respect has intensified with the legalization of abortion, which has subtly taught several generations that if a life isn't wanted or is going to hinder what someone might want to do with his or her own life, that this life can be destroyed. Such disregard for the sanctity of life has reared its ugly head at both ends of the spectrum of life, for the unborn as well as the elderly. The book *Final Exit,* becomes a bestseller, because it speaks of a new philosophy of life—that it is one's right to end life as he or she chooses.

Christians see life differently. They see all of life as precious, from that of the unborn to that of the most aged person, because life is God-given. Discuss with the person sitting next to you the following questions:

1. What are God's instructions concerning the elderly?

a. Leviticus 19:32

b. Psalm 71:9

c. Psalm 92:14–15

d. 1 Timothy 5:4

2. Does your congregation honor the elderly in any special way during the year? When someone in the congregation hits his or her 80th birthday, does the congregation sing "Happy Birthday" after one of its worship services, or is it mentioned in the newsletter?

3. Growing old is not an oversight on God's part. Too often, people challenge God's wisdom, saying, "I don't know why God doesn't take me home." But God doesn't make mistakes. In what ways did God use some of His elderly saints?

a. Moses (Exodus 3:1, 8, 10)

b. Jonah (Jonah 3:1–3)

c. Sarah (Genesis 18:9–10)

THE AGING OF THE CHURCH

Altogether, Methuselah lived 969 years, and then he died.
(Genesis 5:27)

Low birth and death rates have caused an aging not only of America, but also its churches. As the general population grows older, so the population within the church grows older. The evidence comes in the way of statistics:

THE PROPORTION OF MEMBERS 50 YEARS OF AGE OR OLDER		
	1957	**1983**
Episcopalians	36%	46%
Methodists	40%	49%
Lutherans	36%	45%
Presbyterians	42%	49%
Baptists	33%	40%

(From "The Proportion of Members Fifty Years of Age or Older" in AMERICAN MAINLINE RELIGION by W.C. Roof and W. McKinney. Copyright © 1987 by Rutgers, The State University.)

1. Get a copy of the demographics of your own church from either the pastor, the membership secretary, or whoever might have such information. What proportion of your membership is 50 years of age or older? After studying the demographics of your church, what conclusions might be reached, if any?

a. If the trend continues, what does the future of your congregation look like?

b. In what age category are the largest percentage of people?

c. Do you have programs established in your congregation that meet the needs of all ages in your congregation?

d. What might be some of the special needs of the people in the group 50 years and over? What programs do you have available for these people and how do the programs help meet their needs?

2. As more people live longer, more and more families become "sandwich" families, families who try to raise their own children while caring for their aging parents. Can you identify any "sandwich families" in your congregation? What special needs might they have?

GRANNY DUMPING

Recently, newspapers have reported a new trend called "Grannie Dumping." The primary caregivers who "grannie dump" simply get so emotionally spent or financially strapped, they feel there is no alternative but to abandon their responsibility. For example, an aged grandfather was found wandering around at a dog racing track in Florida after being abandoned by his children. His children had sought help from different agencies, but found there was little or no help available. Physically, emotionally, and financially drained, they saw no alternative.

Some observers estimate that there are approximately 1.5 to 2.5 million primary caregivers of incapacitated, aged parents (meaning they are unable to do 3 of the 5 necessary functions: bathing, eating, moving, communicating, and going to the bathroom).

Though the idea of abandoning an aged parent seems appalling, it is a reality and a challenge the church must meet. There are in every congregation primary caregivers who may be crying out for some help, some respite, for a fellow Christian who might care enough to say, "Let me watch your mom for the weekend while you and your husband get away."

ANALYZING THE HEALTH
OF YOUR OWN CONGREGATION

Two are better than one, because they have a good return for their work:
If one falls down, his friend can help him up. But pity the man who falls
and has no one to help him up! Also, if two lie down together, they will
keep warm, but how can one keep warm alone?" (Ecclesiastes 4:9–10)

A favorite hymn is entitled "Blest Be the Tie That Binds":

Blest be the tie that binds
Our hearts in Christian love;
The fellowship of kindred minds
Is like to that above.

We share our mutual woes,
Our mutual burdens bear,
And often for each other flows
The sympathizing tear.

Though the words sound good, the more important question is this: "Are the words true about your congregation?" Do they correctly describe the picture of most congregations? Discuss the following questions in small groups.

1. Consider the results of a survey reported in *A Study of Generations*.

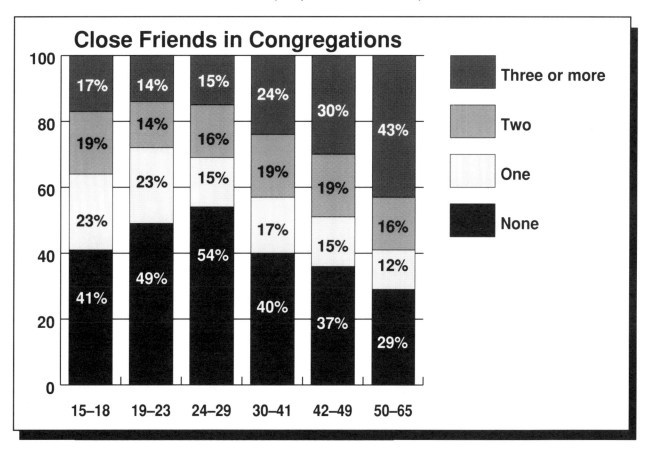

Count the number of close friends you have in your congregation. Total the number of friends identified by the members in your study group, divide by the number of members in the group, and determine if your average is above or below the averages discovered in the study.

2. What were some of the characteristics of the early Christian church according to Acts 2:42–47? Which of the characteristics mentioned are also found in your congregation?

3. What are some of the respective ministries which went on in the early church according to the following passages:

a. 2 Corinthians 1:3–7?

b. Colossians 3:12–17?

c. 1 Thessalonains 5:11?

4. In your opinion, does the church tend to separate families more than "bind" them together?

a. Do we miss gleaning valuable wisdom from other generations when we divide ourselves into specialty groups (e.g., single's group, ages 18–25)?

b. What kind of intergenerational activities take place between the youth and the elderly in your congregation, other than worship?

IMPROVING THE CONGREGATIONAL HEALTH

How good and pleasant it is when brothers live together in unity!
(Psalm 133:1)

It is always easier to identify deficiencies in a congregation than to offer constructive suggestions on how to improve the ministry. Good spiritual leaders in healthy congregations are not only honest and humble enough to admit that ministry can be improved, but also seek God's wisdom and direction in improving their ministry to all ages within the congregation. Discuss in small groups some of the following suggestions for intergenerational ministry in your congregation. Which suggestions might work for you? Why? Why not?

1. Intergenerational gathering for all ages—Make such a happening happen in your congregation by planning a special all-day gathering for grandparents, parents, and grandchildren. Plan activities for each generation. Eat a meal together. Play together! Pray together! Celebrate your oneness in Christ. Consider using *Tell All the World*, an intergenerational Bible study based on the book of Acts (available from CPH).

2. Intergenerational gathering for teenagers and grandparents—ask the teenagers and their grandparents to plan a special time together when both generations can share thoughts on important issues. A committee of some teenagers and grandparents should carefully plan the agenda to include areas of interest for both generations. Both generations might also cooperate in preparing a meal.

3. Special books for the church library—purchase for your church library special books that deal with grandparent-grandchildren issues.

Suggested Books for the Church Library

For Grandparents

The Ten Commandments for Grandparents, by Caryl Waller Krueger (Nashville: Abingdon Press, 1991).

The Joys of Aging, by Martin A. Janis (Dallas: Word Publishing, 1988).

Grandparents, by Charlie Shedd (New York: Doubleday and Company, 1976).

The Blessing, by Gary Smalley and John Trent (New York: Pocket Books, 1990).

For Grandchildren

Ages 3–8

Nana Upstairs and Nana Downstairs, by Tomie dePaola (New York: Puffin Books, 1978).

What Happened When Grandma Died?, by Peggy Barker (St. Louis: Concordia, 1984).

Grandpa and Bo, by Kevin Henkes (New York: Greenwillow Books, 1980).

Ages 8–14

The Trading Game, by Alfred Slote (San Francisco: HarperCollins, 1990).

Black Berries in the Dark (book and video), by Mavis Jukes (New York: Dell Publishing, 1987).

4. An Intergenerational musical—nothing brings people together more than working on a special project such as a minimusical. As you prepare, plan times to eat together, laugh together, and celebrate together.

Family Choir

For a creative and fun idea, ask the choir director to try a "family choir." Who sings in the choir? Eileen Ritter, an expert in the field, answers, "Children—usually first-graders or older—along with at least one adult family member—parents, grandparents, adult brothers or sisters, even godparents." This affords the opportunity for families to participate together in worship. For more information contact Eileen Ritter, 17263 Buchanan, Grand Haven, MI 49417. She's tried it and it works. She'll suggest collections and individual anthems suitable for family choirs.

---

5. Planting a community garden—"All the believers were together and had everything in common" (Acts 2:44).

Purchase or rent a "common ground," where grandparents and grandchildren in the congregation can plant a garden together. Part of the fun is planning the garden before you actually begin planting and harvesting! Get together to decide what you're going to plant. Anticipate what the fresh radishes will taste like! How will you get rid of the nasty weeds that sprout? Grandparents can teach special gardening techniques to grandchildren. Plant the garden together, and then spend time working side-by-side in the garden. Talk about the lady bugs you discover on the potatoes and describe the juicy strawberries as you eat them together! Harvest the crops together. Why not set aside a certain portion of the crop to give away to needy families in the community? When you deliver these special vegetables and produce to the needy, make sure the children accompany you. Why not even can or freeze some of the vegetables to be given away in a special Christmas basket to the needy?

6. Intergenerational day care —instead of having just a day care center for children, include one for the elderly as well. Then combine the two for some of the activities and learning.

7. Sharing skills—schedule a special day when older teenagers and the elderly in the congregation share skills (e.g., a teenager might explain how to work a computer; an elderly person might explain how to crochet).

8. Storytelling in the church nursery—instead of just having the children play in the nursery while church is going on, let it be a time to learn some Bible stories told by the most seasoned and best storytellers in the congregation, the elderly. Schedule a different storyteller for each service. Include the grandfathers!

9. Exchange of services—bring the golden ager's group (or whatever your special group for 50 and over might be called) and youth group together. Ask each group to designate special needs they have (e.g., grandparent might need someone to go shopping for her; a grandchild might need special tutoring), asking each member of the group to participate in helping meet the designated needs.

10. Grandparent/grandchildren camping trip—plan a summer camp for just grandparents and their grandchildren. Plan programs that will open windows for each generation, opportunities for each generation to have one-on-one contact with one another.

11. Adopt a grandparent—ask each Sunday school class to adopt a grandparent(s). Once a month, invite the grandparent to visit the class. The grandparent may tell the Bible story or help with some special craft project. Celebrate birthdays and remember each other in special ways at times during the year. Pray for one another.

12. Kite building and flying—plan a special time to build kites. Then plan a day trip to a special place where you can fly the kites. Take a picnic basket along!

13. Fishing Trip—grandparents make plans to take their grandchildren fishing. There should be a training meeting (where the grandchildren are taught how to bait hooks, etc.), the fishing trip itself, and, of course, the special fish fry afterwards!

14. Adopt a nursing home—have the Sunday school adopt a special nursing home to visit occasionally. At Christmas, carol up and down the halls. At Easter, deliver a special Easter basket. If possible, plan an activity where the children and patients have some physical contact (e.g., holding hands). Some children believe that old age is contagious, something you can "catch." Show them differently!

15. Photo sharing—every household has photos that have never been labeled or preserved properly. Arrange a night when people, young and old alike, bring their photographs to the church, where a professional photographer or someone who knows how to preserve family history through photos, teaches everyone how to best label and preserve these family heirlooms. Inform everyone that toward the end of the evening each generation will be asked to share with others some of their photos and the stories behind them.

16. Make a video—plan a special intergenerational night or day event, inviting entire families (every generation, even if they don't belong to your church). The event might include a picnic and intergenerational games, or it might feature popcorn, soft drinks, and an evening of watching videos. While the families are having fun watching videos, individual families are called into a special room to make their own family video. In every congregation there is someone who is an expert with a video camera. Ask if he or she will spend 5–10 minutes with each family, making a special video of them. As the video is being made, ask someone to interview each member of the family to help facilitate open and honest sharing about family history and memories (including the youngest). At the end of the evening, present each family with a copy of the tape.

17. Serve as surrogate grandparents and grandchildren—separated by thousands of miles, many grandchildren and grandparents find themselves wishing they had grandchildren or grandparents nearby "with skin on!" Identify these people in your congregation. Ask them if they would like to adopt surrogate grandparents or grandchildren. If so, match them with each other.

Choose 2–3 of these suggestions and consider implementing them in your congregation. Invite your pastor and some of the members of the board of elders to discuss with you what intergenerational activities might take place to better bring together the different generations represented in your congregation.

PROGRAMS   STRATEGIES IN ORDER TO MAKE IT HAPPEN

1._____   _____

     _____

     _____

     _____

2._____   _____

     _____

     _____

     _____

3._____   _____

     _____

     _____

     _____

A touching story comes out of a small Kansas farming community. A mother's small toddler wandered away from the house she rented. In back of the house were hundreds of acres of overgrown, weed-covered fields.

Word of the child's disappearance spread quickly throughout the small community. Within an hour, dozens of neighbors showed up at the woman's house to aid in finding her daughter.

Night had already set in. The weather forecaster predicted below freezing temperatures. For hours, everyone searched diligently for the lost child, until the entire community was combed.

Toward morning, more than a hundred men and women joined hands to search the fields directly behind the house. Within a matter of minutes the child was discovered. The child had fallen in a small ravine and had died of exposure.

As he carried the body to the house, a tear-filled neighbor kept saying to himself and others, "If only we had joined hands sooner. If only we had joined hands sooner."

CLOSING LITANY

Leader: Lord God, for the many generations represented in our congregational family,

Participants: We thank You.

Leader: We confess, Lord, that we often fail to respect one another as You tell us in Your Word, to not look down on someone because he is young and to respect the elderly;

Participants: Forgive us, Lord.

Leader: As we analyze the ministry of our congregation, help us to be more than faultfinders. Help us to be constructive in planning and orchestrating programs that will help us bond together as a family. . .

All: And, thus, make our song more than words: [*sing or speak*]

> Blest be the tie that binds
> Our hearts in Christian love;
> The fellowship of kindred minds
> Is like to that above.

> We share our mutual woes,
> Our mutual burdens bear,
> And often for each other flows
> The sympathizing tear.

Leader: Amen. It shall be so.

Shirley Haley/ SUNRISE/TRINITY

Strix Pix

God is not a subservient genie who comes out of a bottle to sweep away each trial and hurdle which blocks our path. Rather, He offers us His will for today only. Our tomorrows must be met one day at a time, negotiating with a generous portion of faith.

—James Dobson

Chapter 6

DIFFICULT QUESTIONS FOR GRANDPARENTS

"INTO EVERYONE'S LIFE SOME RAIN (WILL) FALL"

When King David was old and well advanced in years, he could not keep warm even when they put covers over him. (1 Kings 1:1)

"How long has your husband been retired?"

Reprinted with permission from The Saturday Evening Post © 1989

People seem to always be anticipating something better around the corner! "When I graduate from college, then . . . !" "When I buy my first house, then . . . !" "When I become vice-president of the company, then . . . !" "When I retire, then . . . !" But with each stage of life, there are new problems, new concerns. People work a lifetime to retire, but after they do, new problems arise:

"We moved to Florida, 2,000 miles away from our children and grandchildren, and, despite the fact that the new Leisure World we live in has plush golf courses and bridge throughout the night, we feel lonely without the rest of our family."

"We sacrificed to raise our children in the best neighborhoods, made sure they've had the best education, gave them a rich spiritual background, taught them to be independent, and yet, both of them seem to have gotten off on the wrong track somewhere along the line. They're both divorced. One is living with his girlfriend, refusing to pay child support for his two children left behind from the last marriage, which has made our daughter-in-law resent us. She refuses to even talk to us, much less to allow our grandchildren to talk to us."

"My son is married, but he and his wife say they don't want children. They say they don't want to bring a child into this world, because it's not fair to the child. I would love to have a grandchild, but every time I say anything to him, he gets angry and tells me to mind my own business."

The reality is, as long as we live on this earth, there will be problems.

1. How is life seen from the human perspective (Ecclesiastes 2:17–23)?

2. Problems come with sin.

a. What is the wages of sin according to the apostle Paul in Romans 6:23?

b. In contrast, what is the gift of God?

c. What did Jesus do to set us free from sin and its problems (John 3:16)?

3. Sometimes Christians forget who they are and to whom they belong. They are "new creations" (2 Corinthians 5:17).

They have been resurrected along with Jesus! Examine the promises Christians can confidently claim:

a. Romans 6:3–4

b. 2 Corinthians 12

c. Philippians 4:13

d. 2 Peter 1:4

These verses give the promise that God places in His people special reservoirs of strength to cope with whatever comes along in life. Yes, even difficulties and problems we may face as grandparents. We are resurrected with Christ to new possibilities. In the midst of our tears, nerves, and head-aches, F's, minuses, and zeroes, we are given hope. In the midst of "don't" and "I can't" and "I won't," there is a "yes" and "you can" and "you will."

4. Though, as citizens of this earth, we will never be entirely free from problems, what are we promised as future residents of heaven in Revelation 21:4?

BEATING THE ODDS

***For I, the Lord your God, am . . . showing love
to a thousand generations of those who love me.*** (Exodus 20:5–6)

Helen Romero was trapped for hours between the car door and a tree, after the car she was riding in crashed and rolled down a 500-foot embankment. For the next four months Helen lay in a coma in the Denver Hospital. A brain injury left her helpless with no sight, no speech, and no hearing. Her family was told there was little hope of her recovering.

*Two Miracles: Grandma Helen along with Laura Anne
(and Grandpa, too)*

Helen's mother, Faith, visited her every day from their home in Fort Lupton. During these visits, her mother would say, "I'm sure her eyes follow me as I cross the room," or "I could feel a slight contact when I held her hand." The nurses and doctors would shake their heads and answer, "No, Mrs. Romero, we have tried every test. There just is no reaction." Aside, they confided, "It is just wishful thinking on the mother's part."

Faith Romero never ceased believing that God could bring her daughter out of the coma. Every day her mother would visit her, talking to her even though she never responded.

Since the doctors concluded that Helen would "be as a vegetable" the rest of her life, they recommended she be put into a state mental institution, where the necessary basics would be provided to her. Faith continued to visit her daughter, as often as she could, even though, because of the distance, she could come only once a week. With each visit, she talked to her daughter and prayed for her, confident that God would perform a miracle.

One day, as her mother was visiting her, Helen unexpectedly awakened. She opened her eyes and nodded her head. After physical and speech therapy, Helen Romero went home, defying all the odds once given her. The doctors told Helen, though she could live a normal life upon returning home, because of internal scarring due to the accident, she would be unable to have children.

Four years later, despite what the doctors said, Helen and her husband had the first of three children.

Miracles continued to occur in Helen's family. Thirty seven years later, Kristi, Helen's daughter, conceived and had a one-in-a-million baby.

Kristi, a kidney dialysis patient, was told she would be unable to have children, because of the steroids and other drugs she was taking, as she

71

prepared herself for a possible kidney transplant. Even if she conceived, doctors told her she would miscarry. Doctors quoted statistics, stating that there had only been a few babies in recorded history born to patients on dialysis, and several of those had been born blind. Kristi, however, had the faith of her grandmother, Faith, and her mother, Helen, trusting that God could overcome any medical odds.

A One-in-a-Million Baby

On Dec. 18, 1991, Laura Anne, a healthy baby girl, was born to Kristi and Kenneth Reid. Kristi had beat the odds, one-in-a-million, just as her mother had.

Faith, Helen, Kristi, Laura Anne—four generations who have seen God's miraculous work in overcoming some of the most difficult obstacles life could present—four generations who continue to prove God's promise, "If God is for us, who can be against us? He who did not spare His own Son, but gave Him up for us all—how will He not also, along with Him, graciously give us all things?" (Romans 8:31–32).

WHEN GRANDPARENTS AND GRANDCHILDREN ARE SEPARATED BY MILES

I long to see you, so that I may be filled with joy. (2 Timothy 1:4)

It's no longer easy to go "over the hills and through the wood, to grandmother's house," because grandmother doesn't live "over the hills and through the wood." Neither does she live in a house. She lives in a condominium, a special condominium where children and pets aren't allowed! It's the rules she agreed to when she moved to "Leisure Paradise," 2,000 miles away from her family. When you try to reach her by telephone, you can't, because she's not home; she's out dancing the polka with her new-found "Leisure Paradise" boyfriend.

Things have changed in America. Many elderly are living longer, healthier lives. And they're moving to the Sunbelt—California, Nevada, Arizona, Florida, New Mexico. Despite the fact that Grandma has found a new home and enjoys it, she misses her family, especially her grandchildren back in Minnesota. Her question becomes, "How can I, a long-distance grandparent, keep in touch with my grandkids?"

1. Brainstorm with the person next to you. List 3–5 suggestions on how long-distance grandparents might stay in touch with their grandchildren.

a. _____

b. _____

c. _____

d. _____

e. _____

2. Which of the following suggestions do you think might work for you if you're a long-distant grandparent?

Be creative in communicating with your grandchildren. Letter-writing and telephoning may have been the most common ways of communicating years ago, but times have changed. There are new and exciting ways of communicating that can really help long-distant grandparents. Statistics point out that nearly every home has at least one VCR. More than likely your grandchildren have one or more in their home. Why not make a video for your grandchildren? If you don't have a video camera, odds are that someone down the street does and would be happy to let you use it or tape the recording for you.

Invite your grandchildren to send a videotape back to you. If you don't have a VCR, you might need to go out and buy one, but it would be a good investment.

Another excellent way of communicating is by using cassette tapes. Even your youngest grandchild may own a cassette player. How about recording a story for her? When you send the tape, send the storybook along so that she can follow along, looking at the pictures, as she listens to the tape.

When you send your tape, include a blank tape, asking the grandchild to send a message back to you. Include a self-addressed envelope with postage already on it.

3. Don't forget the traditional ways of staying in touch with your grandchildren—letter writing and telephone. Write letters to each grandchild, not to the family in general or to the grandkids. When telephoning, don't simply ask to talk to your grandchild for a few seconds, but make her feel important by calling and talking exclusively to her!

Don't depend on secondhand reports about the grandchildren from the parents. Parents have a tendency to report only the grandchildren's achievements. Bonding between grandparents and grandchildren takes place best when grandparents and grandchildren have open and honest communication with each other, sharing moments of joy as well as sorrow!

When making your telephone call, decide before you call, what kind of things you're going to ask the grandchild. Ask questions that will open avenues to good communication, beyond simply asking only questions that require a yes or no answer.

4. Periodically, send special gifts. Sometimes, the gift is most meaningful when it's a favorite keepsake such as a broach out of Grandma's jewelry box.

5. Spend some special time together during summer or holiday vacation. Plan it far enough in advance so that the parents and grandchildren can make the necessary plans. The secret is not necessarily what you do, it is that you do something, together!

6. Send a large map of the United States (or of the world) to your grandchild. Tell him to post it in his bedroom (only if Mom says it's okay). As you travel, ask him to follow you on the map as you send letters and cards describing the different things that you are seeing in different locations.

WHEN GRANDPARENTS AND GRANDCHILDREN ARE SEPARATED BY DIVORCE

If it is possible, as far as it depends on you, live at peace with everyone. Do not take revenge. *(Romans 12:18–19)*

More and more grandparents and grandchildren are being separated because the grandparents' children divorce. In some states, there are as many divorces each year as there are marriages. The average divorce rate throughout the United States is one divorce for every 2.8 marriages. In some of the nastier divorces, the children are used as bargaining chips or used to get even.

Before 1965, the courts would not interfere, letting the parents decide if and when the grandparents got to visit their grandchildren. In the last 25 years, almost every state has adopted legislation addressing grandparents' rights. Since most of the states have laws which give grandparents the right to sue for visitation rights, it would be wise for grandparents who seek visitation to seek out a Christian attorney who might clarify the laws of their state.

Agree or Disagree

Discuss in your small group the following statements.

1. When you take sides in a divorce, you may be ostracizing yourself not only from your in-law(s), but also from your grandchildren.

2. Despite the fact that one of the parties may be errant in the marriage, it is important that grandparents display a Christ-like love toward both parties, a love that is not based on one's behavior.

3. Instead of divorce separating grandparents from their grandchildren, it should be a time of special bonding between grandparents and grandchildren, because grandparents can provide continuity and stability for their grandchildren.

4. Grandparents should not try to negatively influence the grandchildren against one of the parents even if one of the parents has been rotten in his or her behavior.

5. Grandparents should try to listen to both sides in order to understand why the marriage failed.

6. After a divorce, your relationship with your spouse becomes an important model for your grandchildren.

7. Just because a parent may have been a poor husband or wife does not mean he or she is a poor parent.

WHEN GRANDPARENTS AND PARENTS DON'T AGREE ON HOW TO RAISE CHILDREN

I appeal to you, brothers, in the name of our Lord Jesus Christ, that all of you agree with one another. (1 Corinthians 1:10)

It is not uncommon for grandparents and parents to disagree on how children ought to be raised. Although, they may disagree, grandparents should never try to supplant the parents. For this reason there must be constant communication between the parents and grandparents to clarify for grandparents what the parents expect of their children and from the grandparents. In no way should grandparents undermine the authority of the parents. But what do grandparents do when they disagree with the grandchildrens' parents?

Consider in your small group the following situations, and discuss which ending best completes the statement.

1. Sally's mother has forbidden her to eat candy before dinner. Sally asks her grandmother, "Grandma, can I have some candy?" Grandma answers,

a. "Sure, it won't kill you, but let's not tell your mother."

b. "As far as I'm concerned you could, but you'd better not, because if she finds out, your mother will kill both of us."

c. "No, I think your mother is very wise in not wanting you to spoil your dinner by eating candy."

2. Your grandson, John, is coming to visit you for the weekend. He asks if he can bring his live-in-girlfriend with him. His parents let them sleep in the same bedroom, and so he asks if he and his girlfriend can share the same bedroom when he visits you. You reply,

a. "Sure, why not? If your mother and dad think it's okay, that's fine with us as well."

b. "Of course not! You know you're going to burn in hell for sleeping together before you're married!"

c. "No, I'm sorry, John. We believe God doesn't approve of two people sleeping together before they're married. Don't worry. Your girlfriend can sleep in the extra bedroom, and we'll make up the couch so that you have a nice comfy place to sleep also."

3. Ten-year-old Joshua comes home with his report card just as you arrive for the weekend. You have promised Joshua that you will take him fishing. After his mother and dad see the report card, they tell Joshua they're going to ground him for the entire weekend because of his poor grades. Joshua is devastated. You're also disappointed. Before going to bed, Joshua looks at you and pleads with tears in his eyes, "Grandpa, I wanted to go fishing with you more than anything in the whole wide world. Would you please talk to Dad and Mom before you go to bed to see if you can get them to change their mind?" You agree. Later, when you are alone with his parents you say,

a. "I want you to know I really support you in how you're raising Joshua. He's so blessed to have parents like you. Would you consider changing your mind regarding our fishing trip tomorrow if we could come up with some kind of agreement on how he might improve his grades in the upcoming weeks?"

b. "I think what you did to Joshua and me stinks! You know how much he looked forward to this fishing trip with me. If I'd known this, we wouldn't have bothered to make the trip. Either you let him go fishing with me or we're going back home."

c. "I know you have forbidden Joshua to go fishing with me tomorrow. I'm wondering if it would be all right if we went to the zoo instead?"

WHEN GRANDCHILDREN SEPARATE THEMSELVES FROM YOU BECAUSE THEY FEAR THE EFFECTS OF AGING

The glory of young men is their strength; of old men, their experience.
(Proverbs 20:29, TLB)

A grandmother writes—

> *My teenage grandson avoids us like a plague. It's not that we've been mean to him; in fact, we've been very good to him, but, I think he's fearful of aging. He sees what it's done to us. His grandfather walks with a cane. I'm crippled with arthritis. What do we do?*

If you were his grandparent, what kind of letter might you write him?

HELPING GRANDCHILDREN UNDERSTAND THE MYSTERY OF AGING

It's important to teach our children and grandchildren that aging is a part of life. You don't catch aging from people who are themselves aging. You age because it's what all human beings do. Unfortunately, because aging eventually leads to death, the world we live in extols and worships youth. The world ignores anything that smacks of aging.

We do a grave disservice to our children and grandchildren when we directly or indirectly give negative messages about aging. Negative messages might include comments such as "Getting old is terrible. Don't ever get old"; and "I don't tell anyone my age."

It's important to teach our children and grandchildren to look at what's inside people, as opposed to what's on the outside.

As parents, we also help our children develop a healthier attitude toward aging when we expose them to a variety of senior citizens, not only in the immediate family but in our neighborhood as well.

WHEN GRANDCHILDREN AREN'T BEING TAUGHT ABOUT JESUS

I am not ashamed of the Gospel, because it is the power of God for the salvation of everyone who believes: . . . For in the gospel a righteousness from God is revealed, a righteousness that is by faith. (Romans 1:16–17)

Grandparents not only have the obligation but the wonderful privilege of telling their grandchildren about Jesus. This becomes especially necessary and important if the parents aren't doing it.

Charlie Shedd in his book, *Grandparents,* writes a short essay entitled "Sometimes When It Is Quiet, They Will Even Talk to You about Heaven":

The small boy said it and I was surprised. But I shouldn't have been. Today's young minds, even the youngest, simply won't settle for zero.

Grade school, junior high, high school, and especially in college they're saying, "See what I found in the wastebasket.

"Could it be true?

"Is it possible?

"Does life really go on?

"Wouldn't it be fun if this forever and forever stuff was for me and my friends?"

And who is wise enough to handle these themes enormous? Someone who has had plenty of time to think? Like a grandparent? Will they most likely be heard?

To which there is only one answer. They will. Love and the Lord, and heaven too can have the feel of the real when they come from a grandmother, grandfather.

Timothy was thirteen when his grandmother died. Same one you could ask, "Why isn't milk green?" It's devastating for a boy to lose his best friend at thirteen. Plus it's like a tree going down outside the window for the rest of us.

Cards from many places, letters, phone calls, telegrams. Comforters coming by the dozen. She had so many friends. But the thing which supported us most, all of our family, was this unabashed word from our seventh-grader:

Do you know what I like to think about now? It is how grandma and I would sit and talk about heaven. She talked mostly about seeing grandpa again. And her baby girl. Then we would discuss it. Would she still be a baby or grown now? And do you know what we decided? We decided heaven is how you want it.

Useless wondering? Maybe! Maybe not! Maybe it's one of the best reasons for being a grandpa or grandma.

> *"Sometimes when it is quiet,*
> *they will even talk to*
> *you about heaven."*

(From *Grandparents.* Garden City, New York: Doubleday & Company, Inc., 1976.)

"BUT MY PROBLEM IS DIFFERENT!"
Hear, O Lord, . . . listen to my cry. (Psalm 17:1)

Spend a few minutes reviewing some of the special concerns and problems you face as a grandparent(s). Identify 3–5 problems you may be facing now as grandparents, and quickly jot them down on a sheet of paper. Then discuss these problems in a small group. Pray for spiritual wisdom and insight as you counsel one another.

Perhaps, as you discuss some of your problems or the problems of others, you will see a real need for additional help and support. Identify people in your community who might be able to answer some of your questions (e.g., a Christian lawyer or family and marriage counselor)?

An excellent newsletter for grandparents is, "**Vital Connections: The Grandparenting Newsletter**," published by Arthur Kornhaber, a leading authority on aging and grandparenting. Each newsletter contains valuable information about different areas of grandparenting, offering some very practical suggestions on how to better grandparent. The newsletter can be ordered by writing the Foundation for Grandparenting, Box 31, Lake Placid, NY 12946.

CLOSING LITANY

Leader: Lord God, for the privilege of grandparenting,

Participants: We give You sincere thanks.

Leader: For "showing mercy to a thousand generations," by sending a Savior to redeem generation after generation,

Participants: We give You thanks, O Lord.

Leader: Despite Your faithfulness toward us, we've turned our backs on You, we've sinned, and with sin has come problems, problems not only in our relationship with You, God, but in our relationships with one another.

Participants: Forgive us, Father.

Leader: Too often, because of sin, grandparents and grandchildren fall victims to the tragedy of divorce within families.

Participants: Forgive us, Father.

Leader: Too often, because of sin, we disagree with one another, we do loveless things to one another, with our words we even hurt our children and children's children.

Participants: Forgive us, Father.

Leader: Thank You, Father, we know You do forgive us and resurrect us to new possibilities.

Participants: In the midst of our tears, nerves, and headaches, F's, minuses and zeroes, You give us hope.

Leader: In the midst of "don't" and "I can't" and "I won't," You say "yes" and "you can" and "you will."

Participants: And we will, Lord; we will be better grandparents, with Your power.

All: Amen.

Your needs change as you grow older— so should your Bible study

Life Cycle:
Journey in Faith Bible Studies

Your needs today aren't the same needs you had 15, 10, or even five years ago. To meet these changing needs, you need the guidance of God's unchanging Word.

Whatever stage of life you're in— from young adult through the retirement years—*Life Cycle: Journey in Faith* has a Bible study for you. *Life Cycle* not only leads you to discover life applications from God's Word, but also offers the opportunity to learn and share with others who have the same concerns.

Suggest one of these *Life Cycle* studies as a summer Bible class, for Sunday morning, or during the Advent/Lenten seasons.

Life Cycle studies are great for:
- *adult Bible class*
- *mid-week Bible study*
- *intergenerational Bible class*
- *women's groups*

• • • • Life Cycle Bible Studies • • • •
Leader Guides _____
Student Guides _____

Off and Running! *Ages 20-35*
Leader Guide _____ 20-2334DAAA
Student Guide _____ 20-2335DAAA

Getting It Together *Ages 30-45*
Leader Guide _____ 20-2336DAAA
Student Guide _____ 20-2337DAAA

Recharting the Waters *Ages 40-55*
Leader Guide _____ 20-2338DAAA
Student Guide _____ 20-2339DAAA

Facing Changes *Ages 50-75*
Leader Guide _____ 20-2340DAAA
Student Guide _____ 20-2341DAAA

Are We There Yet? *Ages 75+*
Leader Guide _____ 20-2342DAAA
Student Guide _____ 20-2343DAAA

CONCORDIA ®
PUBLISHING HOUSE

© 1990 Concordia H52768